JUST
Judy

A CITIZEN AND LEADER FOR ILLINOIS

JOSEPH BAAR TOPINKA

HILTON PUBLISHING · CHICAGO, ILLINOIS

Hilton Publishing Company
1630 45th Avenue, Suite B101
Munster, IN 46321
219-922-4868
www.hiltonpub.com

ISBN 978-0-9983282-2-5 (softcover/pbk.)
ISBN 978-0-9983282-3-2 (e-book)

Angela Vennemann, Senior Editor and Design
Megan Lippert, Publisher
Cover art and original artwork by George Lamson
Original photography by James Nosek

Images supplied by the author, except where noted in image credits.

Library of Congress Cataloging-in-Publication Data

Names: Topinka, Joseph Baar, author.
Title: Just Judy : a citizen and leader for Illinois / by Joseph Baar Topinka.
Other titles: Citizen and leader for Illinois
Description: Munster, IN : Hilton Publishing Company, [2017] | Includes index. | Audience: Ages 9 and up.
Identifiers: LCCN 2017023537 (print) | LCCN 2017022541 (ebook) | ISBN 9780998328232 (Ebook (MOBI & EPUB)) | ISBN 9780998328225 (softcover/pbk.)
Subjects: LCSH: Topinka, Judy Baar. | Legislators--Illinois--Biography--Juvenile literature. | Women legislators--Illinois--Biography--Juvenile literature. | Illinois--Politics and government--1951---Juvenile literature. | Politicians--Illinois--Biography--Juvenile literature. | Women politicians--Illinois--Biography--Juvenile literature. | Illinois. Office of the State Treasurer--Officials and employees--Biography--Juvenile literature. | Republican Party (Ill.)--Biography--Juvenile literature. | Czech Americans--Illinois--Biography--Juvenile literature. | Riverside (Ill.)--Biography--Juvenile literature.
Classification: LCC F546.4.T68 (print) | LCC F546.4.T68 T66 2017 (ebook) | DDC 328.73/092 [B] --dc23
LC record available at https://lccn.loc.gov/2017023537

Contents

Understanding the Meaning of the Book Cover

The cover of this book contains a lot of symbolism and meaning. Some of the most important things to Judy Baar Topinka were family, heritage, leadership, civic duty, and life-long learning.

The cover of Just Judy depicts Judy Baar Topinka next to both the **Illinois State Capitol** in Springfield, Illinois and the **Riverside Township Hall** in the Village of Riverside, Illinois. These buildings represent where Judy worked as a public servant for the great state of Illinois. The **village's water tower** is also next to Judy as it is one of the most famous landmarks in the Village of Riverside.

The red and white book title sign represents Judy's campaign posters that she used when running for the offices of Illinois State Treasurer, Governor and Comptroller.

The bunny image on the book's spine and cover represents a silly cartoon character that Judy used to doodle (draw) in letters and materials she created for family, friends, and colleagues who were special to her. When you received a note from Judy with a bunny drawn on it, you knew that Judy really cared about you.

A **rotunda** is any building with a circular or round building design and often is covered by a dome—like many of our U.S. state capitol buildings are designed. It can also refer to a round room inside the building, often which has a circular area cut out of each of the floors inside the building, so that when standing on the ground level, you can look up and see the dome's ceiling. Go to Springfield, Illinois and look up at the capitol's rotunda and you will see the design that is **the border of the book's cover**. Note the historical statues and the plaster bas-relief frieze at the base of the dome showing Illinois history. Do you know the history of your state?

The Illinois and Cook County flags. The flag of Illinois flies over the capitol. The flag of Cook County symbolically flies over the Riverside Township Hall. Judy had great pride in her state flag and understood the symbolism of the flag. When you get a chance, take a look at the Illinois flag and research what each item on the flag represents. The flag of Cook County represents the county in which Judy grew up but it just as easily represents the flag of all 102 counties in Illinois. Judy visited them all many times and she was proud to be one of the only elected officials in Illinois that could claim to have done that. Do you know what symbols are on your county's flag and/or emblem?

SUSANA A. MENDOZA
ILLINOIS STATE COMPTROLLER

November 8, 2017

Dear Reader:

As you read this book, I hope you will find themes and ideas from Judy Baar Topinka's life that will inspire you to learn, grow, and strive to be whatever you want to be in life. If Judy could talk to you through this book, she'd tell you to dream big because you have the power and ability to make your dreams come true. She would tell you that she believes in you. Judy was an inspiration to me. She was my friend and there is always a little of her influence in the way I live my life and in the way I approach civil service.

For those who didn't personally know her, I would ask you to focus on Judy's sense of civility, integrity, ethics, and heritage. She was always decent and kind to people, even those that were unkind to her. She saw everyone as deserving of respect and had "corazón" (heart) for others. If you wanted an honest answer to a question, Judy would never disappoint you. Some would say she was blunt, but that was just Judy's honesty on display. Always true to her word and in her conduct toward her constituents and her community, Judy did not lie, nor did she tolerate those that did. Finally, Judy loved her Czech and Slovak heritage just as I love my Mexican heritage. We are a country of immigrants and immigrant backgrounds, and Judy understood how this made Illinois and the United States great. She embraced and celebrated the heritage of others, and I believe she saw herself as a world citizen, loving diversity in all facets of life.

Judy Baar Topinka was a role model for so many in Illinois. This is especially true of young women who were told there were limits to what they could accomplish because of their gender. In the late 1970's, Judy stood up to those that said she couldn't be an elected official because she was a woman. When she ran for office, many made fun of her. People threw eggs at her house and belittled her and her family. Yet she would go on to win not only her first election, but also many more thereafter. Most of all, she won the hearts of the people of Illinois who counted on her humor and no-nonsense attitude during the best of times and the worst of times. Judy was one of a kind, an Illinois treasure, and is sorely missed.

Que Dios te bendiga, mi amiga Judy. Nos encontraremos algún dia en el mas allá.

"May God bless you, my friend Judy. We shall meet again on the other side."

Susana A. Mendoza
Illinois State Comptroller

100 West Randolph Street, Suite 15-500
Chicago, Illinois 60601-3252
(312) 814-2451

201 State Capitol
Springfield, Illinois 62706-0001
(217) 782-6000

325 West Adams Street
Springfield, Illinois 62704-1871
(217) 782-6084

Just a Child Growing Up

Judy Baar Topinka was not so different from any other kid when she was a child. She grew up in the twentieth century during a very chaotic period for the world, when the entire planet was at war during what is now known as World War II.[1] Judy was born in the city of Chicago,[2] since in the early 1940s there were not many hospitals in the suburban area of Chicago where her family lived. The city and suburbs were both located in Cook County, Illinois,[3] an area abundant in cultural diversity. It was an environment that would have a profound impact on Judy as she grew up.

Judy grew up with her mother, Lillian, her father, William (also called Bill), and her two Czech grandparents, whom she called *Babi* and *Dedi* Shuss. Babi (sounds like bubb-ee) and Dedi (sounds like jed-ee) mean "grandma" and "grandpa" in the Czech language. The last name Shuss (sounds like shoe-es) had no Czech meaning. Judy's grandfather came from the mostly German-speaking region of Sudetenland in the Austro-Hungarian Empire, and as such, Judy always believed the Shuss name was more German than Czech.

Her grandparents were immigrants from what was then the Austro-Hungarian Empire.[4] This region broke into parts after another big war that occurred earlier during the last century, World War I.[5] The areas from which her grandparents and her great-grandparents came were called Bohemia, the Sudetenland, and Moravia, all of which are now located in the Czech Republic.[6] Her grandparents also had family ties to what is now called Slovakia.[7] Her grandparents were grocers after they moved to the United States and owned a neighborhood store on a street corner in Cicero, Illinois, whose customers were Czechs, Italians, Germans, Irishmen, Englishmen, Poles, and other people from various ethnic backgrounds who had settled in the neighborhoods of Chicago and its suburbs.

Judy's mother, Lillian, was a businesswoman working as a Realtor[8] in the Chicago suburb of Berwyn.[9] When Judy's father, Bill, was in Europe during World War II, Lillian was, in

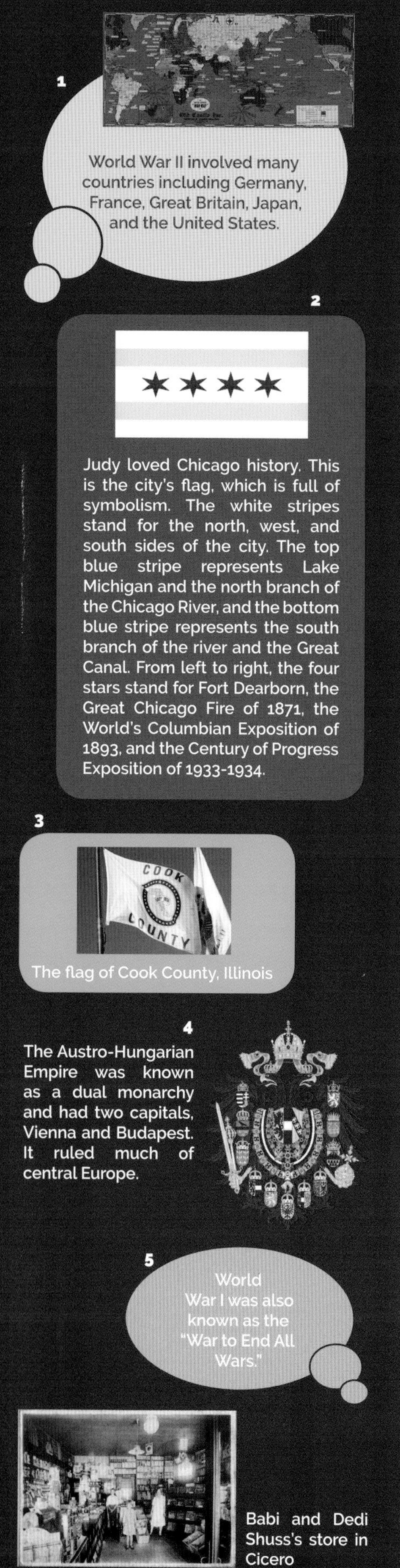

1 World War II involved many countries including Germany, France, Great Britain, Japan, and the United States.

2 Judy loved Chicago history. This is the city's flag, which is full of symbolism. The white stripes stand for the north, west, and south sides of the city. The top blue stripe represents Lake Michigan and the north branch of the Chicago River, and the bottom blue stripe represents the south branch of the river and the Great Canal. From left to right, the four stars stand for Fort Dearborn, the Great Chicago Fire of 1871, the World's Columbian Exposition of 1893, and the Century of Progress Exposition of 1933-1934.

3 The flag of Cook County, Illinois

4 The Austro-Hungarian Empire was known as a dual monarchy and had two capitals, Vienna and Budapest. It ruled much of central Europe.

5 World War I was also known as the "War to End All Wars."

Babi and Dedi Shuss's store in Cicero

effect, a single mother and couldn't always watch over Judy. She was working very hard at selling houses in a business in which women didn't typically work. Back then, women did not work in many fields and were often expected to stay home and raise children. Many people, especially men, made fun of Lillian for working in a "man's" business, and sometimes pranksters even put sugar in the gas tank of her car to slow her down! She couldn't sell homes when her car didn't work. Lillian would eventually tell Judy the stories of opening one of the first woman-owned real estate offices in the western suburbs of Chicago, Baar and Baar Realty,[10] and how difficult it was for a woman to work equally with men. Today we call such conduct gender discrimination. Judy would learn more about gender discrimination firsthand later in her life.

Lillian married Bill in 1942. Bill enlisted in the U.S. Army's Air Corps[11] shortly after the United States went to war with Germany and the other Axis powers. He spent most of Judy's first three years serving in Germany during World War II. Judy, like children of deployed parents in the military today, was happy when her father returned home after the war, but she really didn't know Bill, and there were challenging times of transition when he returned. During the war, Judy had sometimes heard from her father on hardened, plastic records on which her father would record his voice and then send back home to Riverside, the suburb where Judy and her mother lived.[12]

Like so many children living in the United States today, Judy grew up for the first years of her life raised primarily by three people who spoke a language at home other than English, and she learned that other language, Czech, first before she learned English. Also like many children today, Judy spent much of her childhood, even when her father returned from Europe at the end of the war, with her grandparents at their home in Riverside.[13] Judy truly was reared by her grandparents as both her mother and father were very busy selling homes in a post-war, economic boom in the Chicagoland area. The suburbs were growing, and homes were being built at a feverish rate.

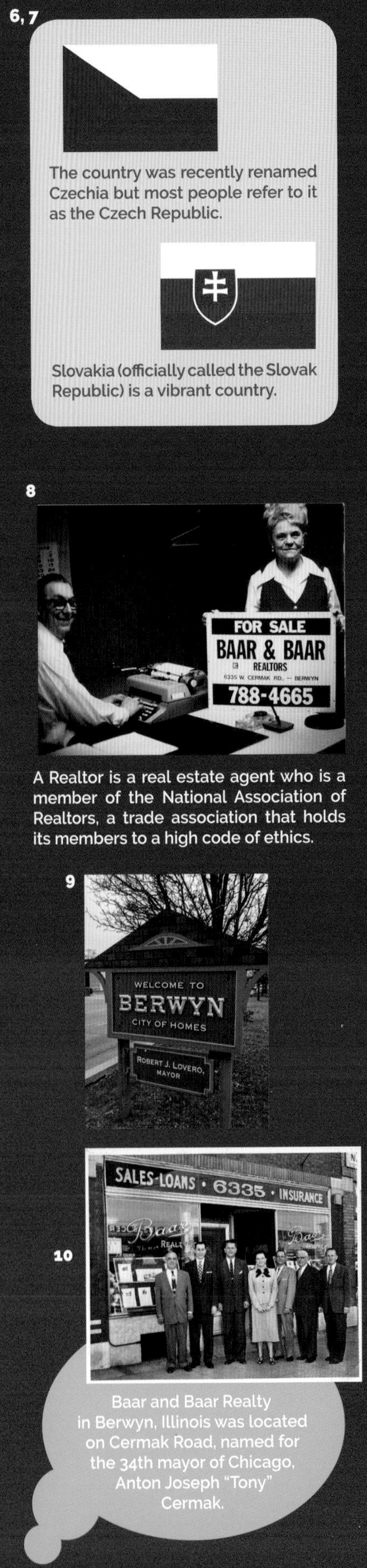

6, 7

The country was recently renamed Czechia but most people refer to it as the Czech Republic.

Slovakia (officially called the Slovak Republic) is a vibrant country.

8

A Realtor is a real estate agent who is a member of the National Association of Realtors, a trade association that holds its members to a high code of ethics.

9

10

Baar and Baar Realty in Berwyn, Illinois was located on Cermak Road, named for the 34th mayor of Chicago, Anton Joseph "Tony" Cermak.

11

The 9th Army Air Force was a unit of the U.S. Army that flew medium-range bombers during WWII. Below are some of the badges that Bill wore during his service.

12

Most people today do not even know what records are and others refer to them as "vinyls." But back in the 1940s, they were the only way to get voice messages to family members. These records would be carried along with mail on ships traveling the Atlantic Ocean. Today we call such mail "snail mail" because it is slower than email or texting. In the 1940s, it took days for ships to move mail back and forth between Europe and the United States—assuming the ships were not sunk by German submarines known as U-boats. There was no Internet or even practical, long-distance phone service between Europe and the United States, so it was difficult for Judy to learn about her father before he returned.

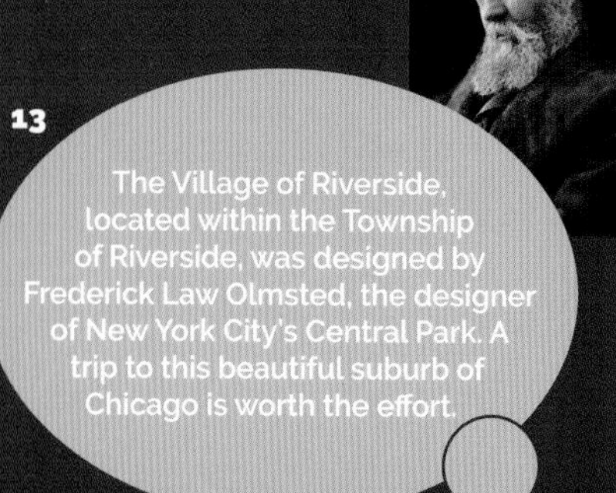

13

The Village of Riverside, located within the Township of Riverside, was designed by Frederick Law Olmsted, the designer of New York City's Central Park. A trip to this beautiful suburb of Chicago is worth the effort.

Judy would live her entire life in Riverside. She would always be influenced by her grandparents' teachings about what was referred to then as "The Old Country," what would become known as Czechoslovakia after World War I. The Old Country was the land that her grandparents had left to take a chance on the promises made by the United States—where they could build a business and raise a family without the harsh restrictions of the Austro-Hungarian rulers. What Judy learned from her Babi and Dedi Shuss forever influenced her appreciation for heritage and the customs of other countries—not only the Czech and Slovak cultures of her ancestors, but those of others as well.

Resources for Further Research

Visit these websites for local information:

- Chicago's history: *http://chicagohistory.org.*
- Cook County, Illinois: *http://www.cookcountyil.gov.*
- The City of Berwyn: *http://www.berwyn-il.gov.*
- The Town of Cicero: *http://www.thetownofcicero.com.*
- The Village of Riverside: *http://www.riverside.il.us.*

These sites have country information:

- The Czech Republic: *http://www.czech.cz/en/Home-en.*
- The Slovak Republic: *http://www.slovak-republic.org.*

For great historical resources, visit:

- The History Channel's website on World War II: *http://www.history.com/topics/world-war-ii/world-war-ii-history.*
- The New World Encyclopedia's entry on the Austro-Hungarian Empire: *http://www.newworldencyclopedia.org/entry/Austri-Hungary.*
- The Wall Street Journal, which presents 100 legacies of World War I in remembrance of the 100th anniversary of the war: *http://online.wsj.com/ww1.*
- Chicago's Museum of Science and Industry. No trip there would be complete without a visit to the U-505, one of the only preserved U-boats from WWII on display to the public: *http://www.msichicago.org/explore/whats-here/exhibits/u-505-submarine.*

To learn more about the real estate profession, visit the National Association of Realtors at *http://www.realtor.org.*

Civics Project Ideas and Classroom Learning Activities

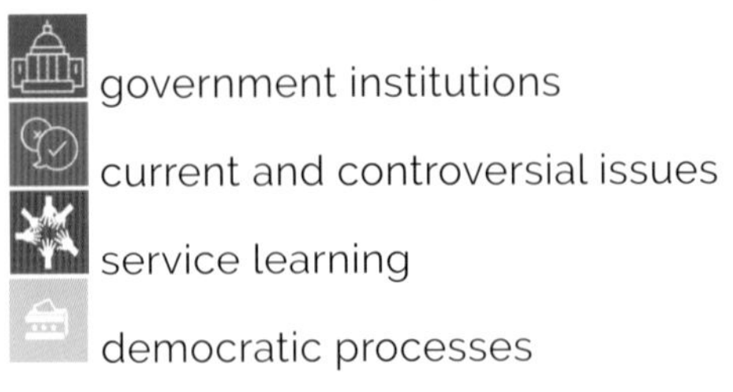

Key Concepts:

- Immigration
- Heritage

- Military Service
- Global Conflicts
- Gender Roles

Chapter 1 Classroom Activities (Teacher):

- Have students research their community, its history, population, demographics, geography, size, climate, city leadership and government, education, etc.
- Ask students to ask family members about family heritage and when their first relatives emigrated to the United States.
- Ask students to speak to family members about whether their relatives served in World War I, World War II, or any other armed conflict such as in Korea, Vietnam, Iraq, or Afghanistan. Back in the classroom, invite students to speak about those in their family who served in the military, when they served, where they served, and what they did.
- Ask your students about the challenges and importance of military service and the sacrifices made by veterans.
- GRADE 6: Create with your class a list of 30 different jobs. Then ask students to describe who typically performs each of those jobs. Discuss how men and women in the past were perceived as being good at or meant for only certain types of work roles because of their gender. How have society and gender roles of the past changed?
- GRADES 7–8: Task class members with finding statistics on the Internet about what percentage of their community is made up of recent immigrants and then telling from what parts of the world those immigrants came. Discuss with students ways they can learn more about those parts of the world so that they can better relate to those new members of the community.

Chapter 1 Essay Topics (Student):

- GRADES 4–5: Imagine your parents were immigrants (define "immigrant"). How might your life be different if they did not immigrate to the United States and to your local community?
- GRADE 6: If you could live anywhere else in the world, where would you move to? Describe what your new life might be like there. Use the Internet to learn more about your new home: its geography and nearby countries, climate, location in proximity to the United States, culture and customs, laws, type of government, currency (define "currency"), job opportunities, education, religion, and other aspects of life that may be important to you such as the cost of living, unemployment rates, and access to healthcare.

Lessons for Life at an Early Age

Life was full of lessons for Judy when she was young, just like it is for all of us. Judy was surprised to learn when she was about 5 or 6 that her mother had been divorced before meeting and marrying her father, Bill.[14] Lillian was a woman more fitted for the late twentieth century or the early twenty-first century than the 1940s. Women then simply did not get divorced, even if they weren't happy in their marriages. But Lillian was not a person who liked remaining unhappy. Lillian was unhappy in her first marriage, so she divorced her husband.

Lillian met Bill Baar during a theatrical performance in the auditorium of the Township Hall in Riverside.[15] Television had not yet been invented, and the Internet wasn't even a dream in anyone's mind. Instead, people often went to auditoriums and dance halls to socialize, dance, or watch performances. Bill eventually proposed to Lillian, who said yes. They married right before Bill "shipped out" for military training.[16] Judy's father regularly told Judy, "I married your mother before I left for the war so I wouldn't lose her." He was right. Lillian and Judy were waiting for him when he returned home in the mid-1940s. And he began selling houses with Lillian in the real estate business that she had started.[17] Judy often said with pride that Bill came back to a ready-made job because of all of his wife's hard work during the war.

Another lesson Judy learned young was to love reading, and that stayed with her the rest of her life. She read many books as a child, especially biographies. Biographies taught her about how great leaders like Napoleon[18] and Queen Elizabeth I[19] took weak countries and made them the strongest nations in the world in their day. She collected many books about these two historic figures.

Judy also learned how to listen well when she was young. Later in life, Judy told her son that she was so good at listening to her voters because of her years listening to all the great shows on the radio during her childhood. Radio shows brought families together in the living rooms of the United States for years,

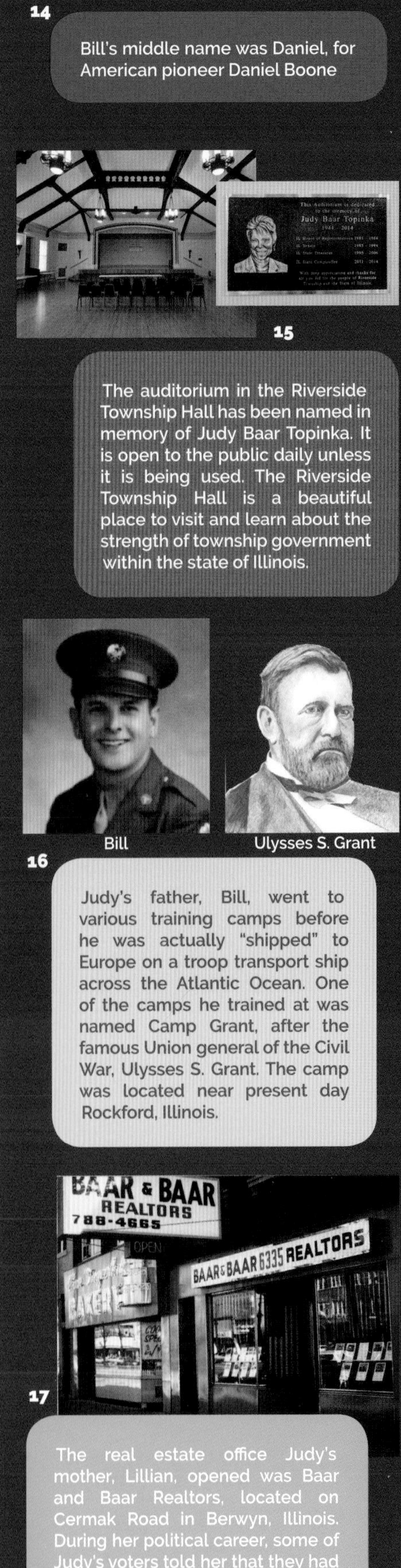

14 Bill's middle name was Daniel, for American pioneer Daniel Boone

15 The auditorium in the Riverside Township Hall has been named in memory of Judy Baar Topinka. It is open to the public daily unless it is being used. The Riverside Township Hall is a beautiful place to visit and learn about the strength of township government within the state of Illinois.

Bill

Ulysses S. Grant

16 Judy's father, Bill, went to various training camps before he was actually "shipped" to Europe on a troop transport ship across the Atlantic Ocean. One of the camps he trained at was named Camp Grant, after the famous Union general of the Civil War, Ulysses S. Grant. The camp was located near present day Rockford, Illinois.

17 The real estate office Judy's mother, Lillian, opened was Baar and Baar Realtors, located on Cermak Road in Berwyn, Illinois. During her political career, some of Judy's voters told her that they had purchased their home or first house through Baar and Baar Realty.

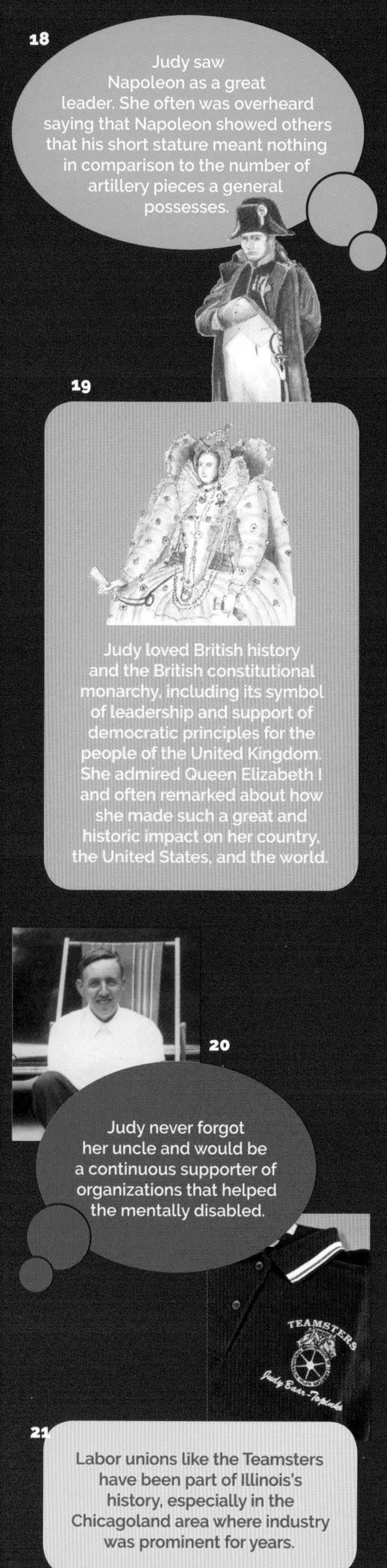

18
Judy saw Napoleon as a great leader. She often was overheard saying that Napoleon showed others that his short stature meant nothing in comparison to the number of artillery pieces a general possesses.
19
Judy loved British history and the British constitutional monarchy, including its symbol of leadership and support of democratic principles for the people of the United Kingdom. She admired Queen Elizabeth I and often remarked about how she made such a great and historic impact on her country, the United States, and the world.
20
Judy never forgot her uncle and would be a continuous supporter of organizations that helped the mentally disabled.
TEAMSTERS
21
Labor unions like the Teamsters have been part of Illinois's history, especially in the Chicagoland area where industry was prominent for years.

both for entertainment and for news. Before the invention of television, Judy often listened for hours with her grandparents. Listening to the radio in addition to reading books encouraged Judy's imagination to grow and develop. She envisioned the Lone Ranger and his companion, Tonto, or the Cisco Kid and his friend, Pancho, chase after criminals in the Old West. Judy loved shows like *The Lone Ranger* and *The Cisco Kid*, and she could listen to them for hours. She also loved mystery books and enjoyed reading the *Hardy Boys* and *Nancy Drew* series.

One of the biggest lessons Judy learned as a child was that people are different, and that everyone should be treated the same no matter their differences. Her Uncle, Jimmy Shuss, was mentally disabled.[20] Judy's grandparents, aunt, and mother would say for years that Jimmy became disabled during birth due to a medical error—as a means to explain their embarrassment over his disability—but the reality was that Jimmy was severely, mentally handicapped due to a condition he developed before he was born. Children taunted and even hit Jimmy at times because he was odd and slow. He was a very big man, but very much a gentle giant. Judy often found herself defending Jimmy, even to the point of fighting other children in the neighborhood who were bigger than she was. She lost many of the fights, but she felt it was her job to protect Uncle Jimmy. Judy's family meant everything to her, and she would stand up for them no matter what it took. Judy would never forget her experiences with her Uncle Jimmy and, as a result, could always relate to the experiences of disabled people fighting for basic rights, including access to employment opportunities and simply being treated fairly. Judy also learned about labor unions and their importance to the community because of her Uncle Jimmy's life. Jimmy's disability kept him from easily finding work, and local employers discriminated against him because of it. Only one organization ever helped Jimmy get a job and that was the Teamsters Union.[21] Its members in the neighborhood helped Jimmy get work picking up garbage in the suburbs of Chicago as a union member. Jimmy was proud to be employed, and the whole family, including his niece, was proud of him as well. Judy didn't know much about labor unions as a child, but for the rest of her life she would not forget her first encounter with the Teamsters and how they helped people.

Something else Judy learned was that she was different. She just didn't fit in with the other girls in the neighborhood. She had the reputation of being a "tomboy," an old-fashioned word used to describe a girl who spent more of her time playing with boys in the neighborhood than with girls. Judy liked sports and she didn't like dolls. She did like stuffed animals, though, and her favorites were a black bear named Cutie and a pink plush dog named Pixie.[22]

Judy's love of animals drew her to horses, and she often dreamed about being a veterinarian, an unusual career choice for a young girl growing up in the early 1950s, as it was a profession in which only men worked. But, if her mother could be a Realtor, Judy could certainly pursue any profession she desired. Many people don't know that Judy had a pet bunny as a girl, and while the name of the bunny has long been forgotten, this bunny meant the world to Judy while she was growing up mostly in her grandparents' home. The bunny lived in the basement but hopped upstairs and watched television with the family.[23] After the Shuss family bought one of the first televisions in the neighborhood, that bunny spent a lot of time watching shows with them. Judy continued to love bunnies forever after. Later in life, Judy acquired a habit of sketching a bunny on correspondence sent to friends.[24]

Judy learned as a young child to appreciate music, which was frequently heard in a Czech household that loved Czech music and polka. Judy and her Dedi would often walk to the Cook County Forest Preserve's National Grove near her grandparents' house on the northwest edge of Riverside on Saturday and Sunday afternoons. At the grove, they could buy and eat homemade potato pancakes, dumplings, sausage, and roast pork; dance; and listen to the sounds of the accordion. Dedi Shuss always brought his metal bucket of Pilsner pivo (the Czech word for beer; sounds like pee-vo). Pilsner pivo is world-famous, and it gets its name from Plzeň, Bohemia, where such beer was first produced in 1842.

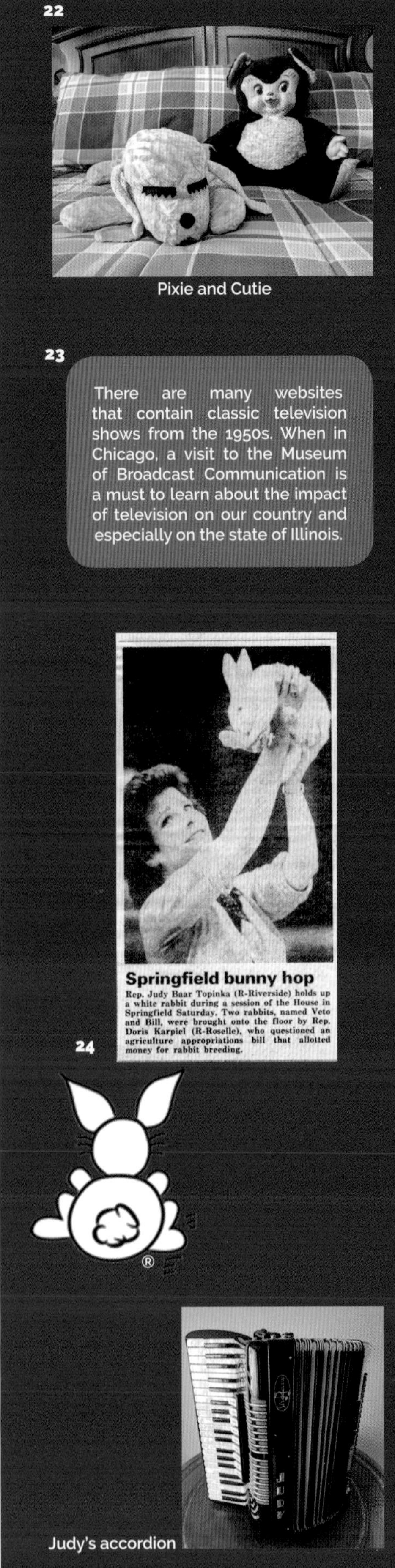
22

Pixie and Cutie

23

There are many websites that contain classic television shows from the 1950s. When in Chicago, a visit to the Museum of Broadcast Communication is a must to learn about the impact of television on our country and especially on the state of Illinois.

24

Springfield bunny hop

Rep. Judy Baar Topinka (R-Riverside) holds up a white rabbit during a session of the House in Springfield Saturday. Two rabbits, named Veto and Bill, were brought onto the floor by Rep. Doris Karpiel (R-Roselle), who questioned an agriculture appropriations bill that allotted money for rabbit breeding.

Judy's accordion

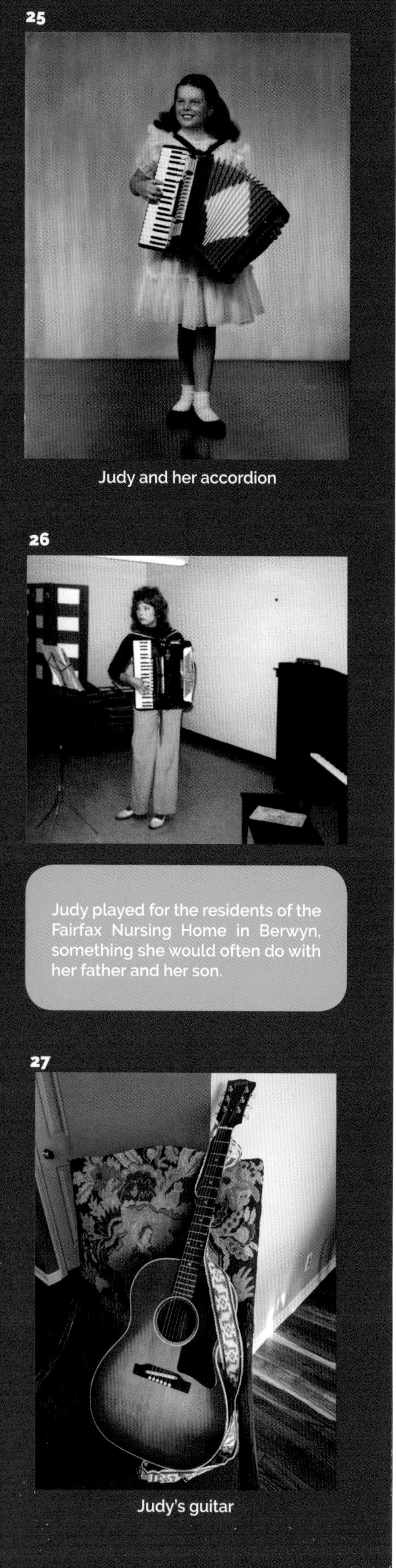

25

Judy and her accordion

26

Judy played for the residents of the Fairfax Nursing Home in Berwyn, something she would often do with her father and her son.

27

Judy's guitar

Judy loved the sound of the accordion, so her parents sent her to accordion lessons and she soon became very good at playing it. Even back then, the accordion was considered a bit of an odd instrument in the United States, and there were not many women who played it.[25] Judy eventually came to play Czech and Slovak music just as well as any seasoned player, and she was frequently asked to come to parties just to play her chosen instrument. Later in life, people knew her as *the politician who played the accordion*—and who made people sing and smile.[26]

Judy's father expected her to also learn the piano, which she did—along with the guitar,[27] though she was never as passionate about those instruments as she was about the accordion. Bill was quite the pianist when he was younger and often played for military officers when he was in Europe during World War II. He used to boast that as a lowly private in the U.S. Army, he was able to get extra rations for his friends on the troop ship going to England because of the show he helped put on for the ship's officers. Bill saw piano in particular, and just playing a musical instrument in general, as critical in any child's upbringing. His ability to play enabled him to do things that others could not, and he likewise expected Judy to use her musical talent to do things that others could not.

Bill was probably right in requiring Judy to study piano, but then Judy's parents and grandparents loved her very much. They, like parents today, only wanted what was best for their daughter and they wanted Judy to have a better life than they'd had. For them, the United States and the state of Illinois gave them a promise of what was often referred to as the "American Dream."

Some say that Judy was different—and maybe she was—but that was not a bad thing. Judy learned Czech and English growing up. She was skilled at listening, reading, and learning from both languages. She knew how to read music and how to play three instruments. She was immersed in culture and heritage. What a wonderful childhood! But she also saw some of the ugly sides of life: discrimination, inequality, and hate. She didn't like what she saw and she never would forget those darker lessons.

Resources for Further Research

For information about Riverside Township:
https://www.toi.org/Townships/Cook_County/Riverside_Township/Riverside-Township.

The Daughters of the British Empire manage charitable activities throughout the United States. For more about them: *http://www.dbenational.org.*

One organization that supports the mentally disabled is Seguin RCA, located at *http://www.seguinrca.org.* Similar organizations located all over Illinois provide individuals opportunities to contribute to their local communities. The Topinka family contributes to this organization and encourages others to support similar organizations within their communities.

Judy had a particular closeness to the International Union of Operating Engineers located in Countryside, Illinois: *http://www.local150.org.* Most unions in Illinois have websites. Explore them and consider whether you may want a career that is unionized. You can also talk to friends and family who are in unions about the importance of unions in their lives.

Learn more about television and radio history at Chicago's Museum of Broadcast Communication: *http://www.museum.tv/index.htm.*

The Cook County Forest Preserves system contains some of the most beautiful forested areas in Cook County, Illinois. Visit one when you can and have a picnic with friends or family. See the website for more information: *http://fpdcc.com.*

A scholarship for college music majors was established in memory of William Baar at Triton Community College. See the website for more information: *http://www.triton.edu/William-Barr-Memorial-Scholarship.*

Civics Project Ideas and Classroom Learning Activities

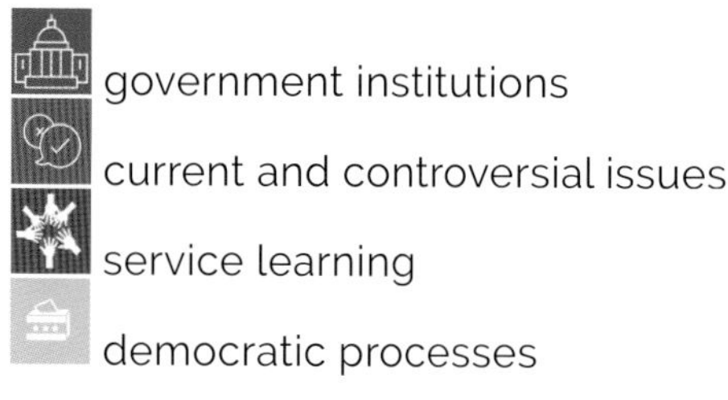

- government institutions
- current and controversial issues
- service learning
- democratic processes
- heritage
- compromise
- leadership
- critical thinking

Chapter 2 Key Concepts:

- Biography
- Hobbies and Extracurricular Activities
- Disabilities Awareness
- Living with Animals
- Music Appreciation

Chapter 2 Classroom Activities (Teacher):

- Ask students to name some extracurricular activities, such as taking piano lessons and playing soccer—the ones they participate in and the ones they are interested in. Discuss as a class the benefits of these activities, what lessons they teach us related to concentration, handling pressure, team work, setting goals, hard work, making mistakes and learning from them, etc.
- Ask students if they could meet anyone from any point in history, who would that person be and why?

Chapter 2 Essay Topics (Student):

- Write about an extracurricular activity you are (or used to be) involved with. How did you feel when you first started that activity? What were your goals? Did you meet them? Why or why not? If you could do that activity over again, what would you do differently?
- Read a biography about someone in history you think is amazing. Write about why you picked that person and what that person inspires you to think about and do in your life.

OFFICE OF THE SECRETARY OF STATE

JESSE WHITE • Secretary of State

Dear Reader,

Judy Baar Topinka was a remarkable and kind individual who held steadfast to her beliefs. Through her words, as well as her actions, she emphasized that we are stronger because of the diversity of our backgrounds, gender, race, heritage and goals. In the next few chapters, I hope you gain perspective about how her education and dedication to community fostered her growth into a statewide leader who gained the trust and loyalty of voters for decades.

Judy and I both served on the House Human Services Committee. She was the ranking Republican and I was the Democratic chairman. Although we were from different political parties and represented different constituencies, Judy and I worked well together and achieved common ground for the entire state of Illinois. I was proud of our work together, and I miss her dearly.

As we live our lives each day, let us remember Judy's wise message – Together we can do great things.

Sincerely,

Jesse White

Jesse White
Illinois Secretary of State

100 W. Randolph, Ste. 5-400,
Chicago, IL 60601

Educating Judy

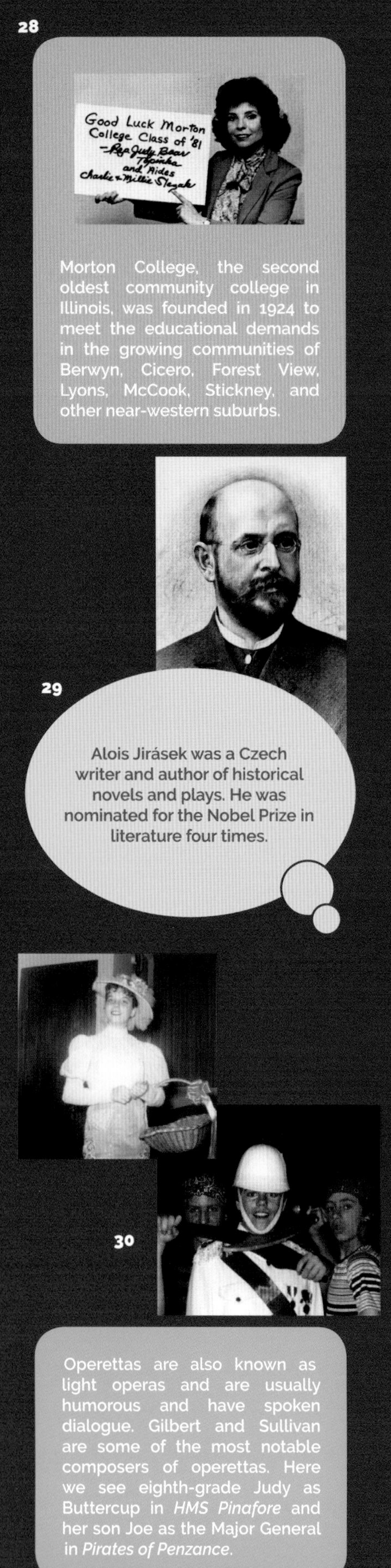

28

Morton College, the second oldest community college in Illinois, was founded in 1924 to meet the educational demands in the growing communities of Berwyn, Cicero, Forest View, Lyons, McCook, Stickney, and other near-western suburbs.

29

Alois Jirásek was a Czech writer and author of historical novels and plays. He was nominated for the Nobel Prize in literature four times.

30

Operettas are also known as light operas and are usually humorous and have spoken dialogue. Gilbert and Sullivan are some of the most notable composers of operettas. Here we see eighth-grade Judy as Buttercup in *HMS Pinafore* and her son Joe as the Major General in *Pirates of Penzance*.

There are places in the world where children unfortunately do not have the chance to go to school. It is a sad reality. When Judy's grandparents came to the United States, they had had very little schooling. They learned mostly from just living their lives from day to day. Judy's parents, as first generation Czech-Americans, had more opportunities. Her father, Bill, was able to get a high school education at Harrison High School in Chicago. He went on to get an education of a different kind through the U.S. Army Air Corps like many young people do today when joining the Army, Air Force, Navy, Marine Corps, or Coast Guard. Little is known about the education of Judy's mother, Lillian, except that she was accepted into Morton College[28] in Cicero, Illinois, and took several college courses there. Lillian saw the importance of a college education even though, at the time, it was usually only men who attended college. Lillian undoubtedly instilled her own drive for education into Judy.

Bill and Lillian Baar insisted that Judy attend Czech school, Ceska Skola (sounds like chess-ska sko-la), in addition to regular school. She attended the Alois Jirásek Czech School[29] every Saturday until she reached high school, an incredible life commitment on her part. There she learned to speak and write Czech better and learned more about her ethnic heritage. During the week, Judy went to the public schools in Riverside. First, she attended A. F. Ames Elementary School because it was very close to where she lived with her grandparents. When she grew older, she attended Riverside Junior High School. She loved her time at Riverside Junior High because her music teacher, Mr. Sheehan, had established a four-year cycle of annual musicals based on Sir William Schwenck Gilbert's and Arthur Sullivan's English operettas: *Patience, The Mikado, Pirates of Penzance,* and *HMS Pinafore.*[30] She loved these operettas, but she especially loved *HMS Pinafore*, in which she had the lead role of Buttercup in her eighth grade year. Her love for the music of Gilbert and Sullivan lasted her entire life. She was especially proud when her son, Joseph, had the lead role as the Major General in *Pirates of Penzance* over twenty years later at the same school.

After grade school, Judy's parents sent her to an all-girls boarding school in Lake Forest, Illinois, called Ferry Hall.[31] It was well known in the Chicago area as a good college preparatory school. Judy missed her parents very much, but she made many friends at Ferry Hall and many would be her best friends for life. She was president of her class once, and later, head of student government, foreshadowing her future career in public office. Judy was always very outgoing and the person her friends would come to with their problems. She did not always have answers, but she went out of her way to help them find solutions, an attribute that would be common later in her life. She was loyal to her friends and would do practically everything to help them in times of need.

Judy loved sports, especially field hockey,[32] which can be a rough game in which players would often take their wooden sticks and slam them into opposing players' shins. She would tell her son years later that games could be brutal. Judy often ended a game bruised, but she also bruised her opponents. She was very competitive, and she got that from her father, who never missed a game even though he had to travel a long distance to be there. Bill inspired Judy to compete intensely in sports just as he had competed as a youth in the Czech-American Sokol[33] (sounds like so-call) program that encouraged physical fitness and teamwork.

Judy was a good writer, and she scored very high on the verbal part of the Scholastic Aptitude Test (SAT) needed to apply for college. Later in life, she told her son repeatedly that she credited her success on the exam and to writing well in general to her classes in Latin at Ferry Hall. Latin taught her how to break words down to understand their meanings. When Judy was accepted by Northwestern University's Medill School of Journalism,[34] she was the first in her family to ever attend a four-year university. Later, she became the first in her family to graduate from a university and receive a college degree.[35]

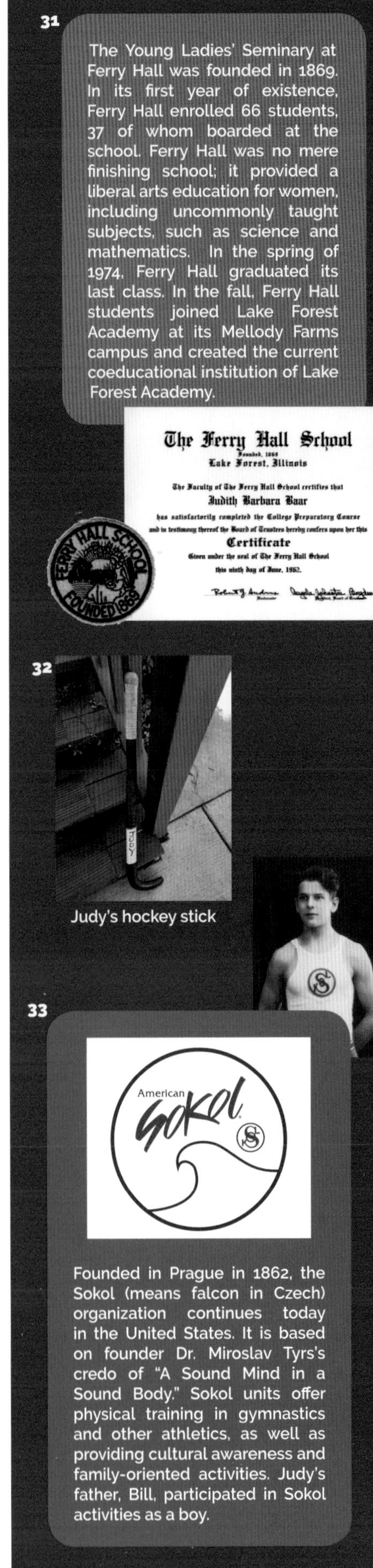

31 The Young Ladies' Seminary at Ferry Hall was founded in 1869. In its first year of existence, Ferry Hall enrolled 66 students, 37 of whom boarded at the school. Ferry Hall was no mere finishing school; it provided a liberal arts education for women, including uncommonly taught subjects, such as science and mathematics. In the spring of 1974, Ferry Hall graduated its last class. In the fall, Ferry Hall students joined Lake Forest Academy at its Mellody Farms campus and created the current coeducational institution of Lake Forest Academy.

The Ferry Hall School
Founded, 1869
Lake Forest, Illinois

The Faculty of The Ferry Hall School certifies that
Judith Barbara Baar
has satisfactorily completed the College Preparatory Course
and in testimony thereof the Board of Trustees hereby confers upon her this
Certificate
Given under the seal of The Ferry Hall School
this ninth day of June, 1962.

32 Judy's hockey stick

33 Founded in Prague in 1862, the Sokol (means falcon in Czech) organization continues today in the United States. It is based on founder Dr. Miroslav Tyrs's credo of "A Sound Mind in a Sound Body." Sokol units offer physical training in gymnastics and other athletics, as well as providing cultural awareness and family-oriented activities. Judy's father, Bill, participated in Sokol activities as a boy.

34

Joseph Medill was a Canadian-born American editor and publisher who from 1855 built the *Chicago Tribune* into a powerful newspaper. He was the grandfather of three newspaper publishers: Robert R. McCormick of the *Chicago Tribune*, Joseph M. Patterson of the *New York Daily News*, and Eleanor M. Patterson of the *Washington (D.C.) Times-Herald*.

35

Northwestern University

ON RECOMMENDATION OF THE FACULTY OF THE
MEDILL SCHOOL OF JOURNALISM
NORTHWESTERN UNIVERSITY HAS CONFERRED THE DEGREE OF
BACHELOR OF SCIENCE IN JOURNALISM
UPON
JUDITH BAAR TOPINKA
WHO HAS HONORABLY FULFILLED ALL THE REQUIREMENTS PRESCRIBED BY THE UNIVERSITY FOR THAT DEGREE
DONE AT EVANSTON ILLINOIS THIS ELEVENTH DAY OF JUNE IN THE YEAR OF OUR LORD ONE THOUSAND NINE HUNDRED AND SIXTY-SIX

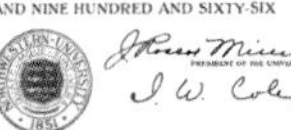

36

These modest homes exhibit elaborate design elements typically not seen in other types of architecture, such as stained glass windows, clay tile roofs, terra cotta, and intricate brick patterns. Many versions of the bungalow have been built around the world since the late 1800s. These homes make up the Central Berwyn Bungalow Historic District, one of the largest such districts in the U.S.

Part of Northwestern University's campus is on the shore of Lake Michigan. Judy loved spending hours on the beach, staring across the water. The view was beautiful. She went there when she wanted to contemplate her life and her future. She knew that journalism was the right fit for her. She was an excellent writer, had a way with words, and was not afraid to ask tough questions. Her parents and grandparents were incredibly proud of her, but Judy felt a little out of place at Northwestern as there were not many women enrolled there. In addition, Judy's family was by no means rich or affluent, and tuition at Northwestern University was expensive. She had been reared in a modest home with two working parents, both Realtors who sold bungalows[36] in Cicero and Berwyn, middle-class suburbs. But Judy learned that she had to go outside her comfort zone and relate with peers and colleagues from different social and economic backgrounds in order to succeed, a lesson she would apply the rest of her life when dealing with people from all over a state as diverse as Illinois.

Resources for Further Research

Learn more about the schools that Judy attended:

- Riverside School District 96: *http://www.district96.org.*
- American Sokol: *http://american-sokol.org.*
- Lake Forest Academy: *http://www.lfanet.org/page.cfm?p=583.*
- Northwestern University's Medill School of Journalism: *http://www.medill.northwestern.edu.*

More information about Morton College, where Lillian took classes, can be found at *http://www.morton.edu.* The Illinois Community College System consists of thirty-nine public community college districts. Find out where your local community college is located as it may offer some great educational opportunities or experiences for you and your family. A scholarship in memory of Lillian Baar was established for female business majors at Morton College.

Boise State's website (*https://diamond.boisestate.edu/gas*) has an incredible archive on Gilbert and Sullivan operettas. Listen to the music that Judy loved!

The "Chicago-style" bungalow is the predominant style of bungalow home found in Berwyn, Illinois, and, according to the School of the Art Institute, Berwyn has the most significant collection of Chicago-style bungalows in the nation. Read more about Berwyn and its bungalows at: *http://www.cityofhomes.org/berwyn-and-the-bungalow.*

Civics Project Ideas and Classroom Learning Activities

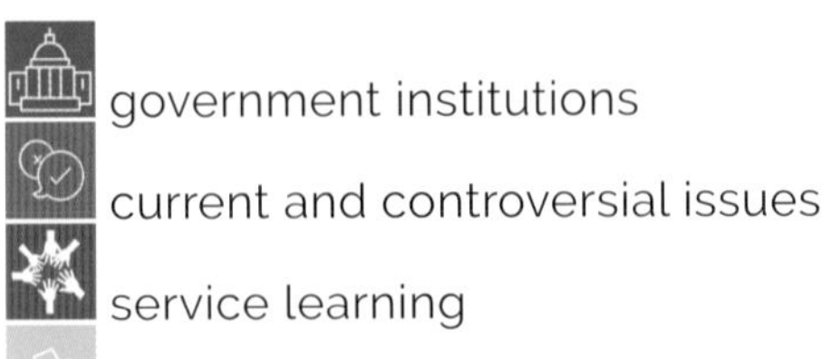

Chapter 3 Key Concepts:

- The path of school, higher education, career
- Pride in heritage
- Competition
- Networking

Chapter 3 Classroom Activities (Teacher):

- Ask students whether or not they want to go to college. If they do, where would they want to go and why? If not, what other options may they pursue?
- Ask students what they want to do when they are older and in the workforce. Use their examples to discuss the different types of training and education necessary for a range of jobs and careers.
- Judy Baar Topinka played field hockey in high school. It taught her about competition. Why is competition so important in life?
- GRADES 6-7: Ask students: 1) Do they think they want to go to college...why or why not? 2) What do they want to do when they are older? 3) What are their favorite subjects in school? 4) What are they good at? Then ...all leading into how we choose paths in life and what the post-HS options are for training, degrees, etc. and how that all feeds into career options. Discuss different career paths driven by those basic academic disciplines, and talk about different college degree programs and technical schools that build on those basic subjects for specific jobs and careers.

Chapter 3 Essay Topics (Student):

- What does your heritage mean to you? Is knowing about it important? How do you learn about it? Are there ways you celebrate it?
- Have you ever competed with or against someone? Why and for what? Did it help you become better in some way than before you competed?
- GRADE 5-6: How do you think education and schooling helped Judy Baar Topinka? How was her education different than yours? Discuss and compare Judy's schooling to yours—in what ways are they different and in what ways are they similar?
- GRADES 7-8: Have you ever heard about the concept of networking with other people? What does it mean and how can you network better at school and college so you meet people and learn how to work with them later in life?

Judy Out in the World

Journalism was a natural fit for Judy Baar Topinka, due in part to her love for the communities in which her parents worked selling homes at Baar & Baar Realty in Berwyn. Judy's mother, Lillian, knew the importance of being good to the community that provided business to the family. Lillian was Judy's greatest mentor.[37] Her mother's community-minded attitude became Judy's attitude for the rest of her life.

Judy began her journalism career as a part-time newspaper reporter at the *Berwyn Life*,[38] where she eventually took a full-time position. The switch to full-time greatly affected the amount of time she could spend with her family, but it allowed Judy to cover more stories in depth. It was the first of many sacrifices that she and her family would endure for years to come on behalf of the public. Community newspapers like the *Berwyn Life* informed people living in the suburbs about the happenings in their immediate surroundings, while papers like the *Chicago Tribune*, *Chicago Sun-Times*, and *Chicago Daily News* focused on city, state, and national issues. Such local newspapers served a niche where Judy, with her community-minded focus, fit in perfectly.

Judy loved being a reporter, and it showed in the way she used words when writing articles.[39] She could put people at ease, but she could also be blunt. That bluntness irritated some but delighted many others who found it refreshing, especially from a woman in a profession dominated by men. Judy followed many of Berwyn's stories, but her favorites by far came from the police and local government beats. A beat is the area of interest or type of story that a journalist follows. She liked to point out how you could tell when it was a slow news day: newspaper editors used crime stories to fill in the gaps. Police reports were normally well written and gave reporters solid information they could use in the newspapers.

Judy considered television news briefly, and even applied for a job with WGN News (Channel 9) in Chicago by sending the station a demonstration video of her conducting an interview

37

A mentor is a person who teaches or gives help and advice to a less experienced and often younger person about personal, professional, and civil development. A mentor can be a teacher, a parent, or a friend, and it is always good to find a mentor or many mentors in life. Congressman Henry Hyde, pictured above, was a mentor to Judy.

38

Berwyn Life used to be located on the corner of Harlem Avenue and 26th Street in Berwyn, Illinois. It was the premier newspaper for Berwyn and Cicero for many years. It was absorbed into the *Suburban Life Newspapers* system that covers all of suburban Chicago today.

39

Berwyn Life, Wed Jan 26, 1972

Medics rate LIFE story best of '71

By SEAN O'GARA

A news feature by Judy Topinka, LIFE features editor, has been awarded the first place Outstanding Medical Feature Award for 1971 by the Illinois State Medical Society, it was announced this week.

Her feature story, "There's New Hope for Heart Victims," appeared first on December 26 in the Cicero, Berwyn and Stickney-Forest View LIFE Newspapers, and subsequently also appeared in all editions of the Suburban LIFE.

BASED on the experiences of Dr. Roque Pifarre, head of cardiac surgery at the Stritch School of Medicine, Maywood, the article stressed his operations on patients in the process of having heart attacks.

Dr. Pifarre is the first surgeon in the Midwest to perform an operation under these circumstances and was successful in saving 11 out of 14 patients.

Presentation of the award, an engraved plaque, will be made on Saturday, May 6, at the society's annual awards dinner in the Playboy Towers Hotel, Chicago.

Judy Topinka

The article has now been submitted by the ISMS to the American Medical Association for consideration in its national Medical Awards Program.

IN ALL, 18 newspapers, television and radio stations received various awards for outstanding coverage of medical and health topics during 1971.

Mrs. Topinka, wife of Joseph Topinka, of Riverside, and daughter of Mr. and Mrs. William D. Baar, also of Riverside, first came to The LIFE as a part-time general reporter in 1966, upon graduation from Northwestern University, Evanston.

She later became education editor, covering the area's various school districts and editing the education pages.

IN 1971 she received a second place award from the Illinois Press Women's Association for technical writing and also earned an honorable mention for "best news story" from the Illinois Press Association.

More recently, she received a Golden Houby Award from the Cermak Road Business Association for her efforts in publicizing last year's Houby Festival.

She is active in the Riverside Junior Woman's Club, Berwyn Business and Professional Women's Club, Northwestern Alumni Association and various other organizations including several Czech groups.

Judy's writing earned her several awards.

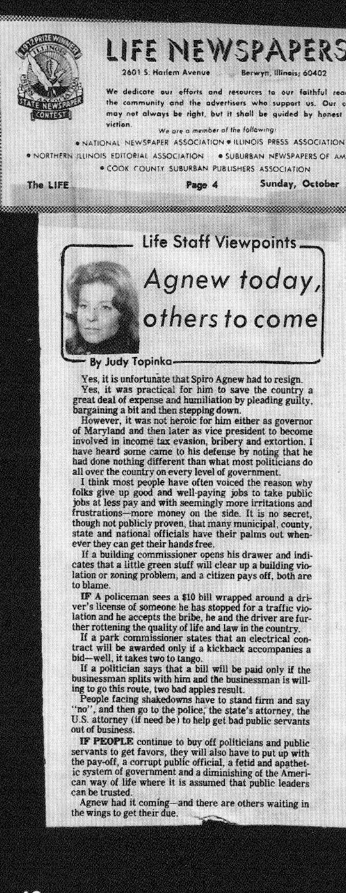

LIFE NEWSPAPERS

2601 S. Harlem Avenue Berwyn, Illinois; 60402

We dedicate our efforts and resources to our faithful readers, the community and the advertisers who support us. Our cause may not always be right, but it shall be guided by honest conviction.

We are a member of the following:

• NATIONAL NEWSPAPER ASSOCIATION • ILLINOIS PRESS ASSOCIATION • NORTHERN ILLINOIS EDITORIAL ASSOCIATION • SUBURBAN NEWSPAPERS OF AMERICA • COOK COUNTY SUBURBAN PUBLISHERS ASSOCIATION

The LIFE Page 4 Sunday, October 14, 1973

Life Staff Viewpoints

Agnew today, others to come

By Judy Topinka

Yes, it is unfortunate that Spiro Agnew had to resign.

Yes, it was practical for him to save the country a great deal of expense and humiliation by pleading guilty, bargaining a bit and then stepping down.

However, it was not heroic for him either as governor of Maryland and then later as vice president to become involved in income tax evasion, bribery and extortion. I have heard some came to his defense by noting that he had done nothing different than what most politicians do all over the country on every level of government.

I think most people have often voiced the reason why folks give up good and well-paying jobs to take public jobs at less pay and with seemingly more irritations and frustrations—more money on the side. It is no secret, though not publicly proven, that many municipal, county, state and national officials have their palms out whenever they can get their hands free.

If a building commissioner opens his drawer and indicates that a little green stuff will clear up a building violation or zoning problem, and a citizen pays off, both are to blame.

IF A policeman sees a $10 bill wrapped around a driver's license of someone he has stopped for a traffic violation and he accepts the bribe, he and the driver are further rottening the quality of life and law in the country.

If a park commissioner states that an electrical contract will be awarded only if a kickback accompanies a bid—well, it takes two to tango.

If a politician says that a bill will be paid only if the businessman splits with him and the businessman is willing to go this route, two bad apples result.

People facing shakedowns have to stand firm and say "no", and then go to the police, the state's attorney, the U.S. attorney (if need be) to help get bad public servants out of business.

IF PEOPLE continue to buy off politicians and public servants to get favors, they will also have to put up with the pay-off, a corrupt public official, a fetid and apathetic system of government and a diminishing of the American way of life where it is assumed that public leaders can be trusted.

Agnew had it coming—and there are others waiting in the wings to get their due.

of a staff member at Brookfield Zoo near the old walrus pool where the late Olga the Walrus lived. Judy often recalled that Olga sprayed her with water during the interview multiple times. But walrus antics did not help Judy get a job at WGN News, and she continued being a local newspaper reporter. She went on to also write part-time for the *Forest Park Review*, a role that allowed her to reach more people in neighboring suburbs and further exposed her to various local governments and their issues. In a short time, Judy became well informed about local government leaders at the municipal, township, and county levels in the near western suburbs. She observed corruption, bureaucracy,[40] waste, and most of all, restrictions on opportunities for women. These observations would influence her ideas about governmental management for her future political career.

Judy briefly worked for the American Medical Association (AMA)[41] in Chicago, which gave her more traditional hours than newsroom work and permitted her to spend more time with her young son and husband. Like many people's work, it was less of a career and more of a job. It also came with a very hierarchical bureaucracy, something to which Judy was not accustomed after the great freedom she enjoyed as a reporter. Working at the AMA taught her lessons about working within a corporate structure as well as a great deal about health care in the United States. She used this knowledge later in life during her tenure on legislative committees regarding healthcare. Going to work at the AMA also taught Judy about the trials and tribulations of riding the Chicago Transit Authority's (CTA) Blue Line. Like many commuters today, Judy came to have a love/hate relationship with the world famous "L" that stayed with her for the rest of her life.[42] The "L" was the most efficient way for Judy to travel to downtown Chicago, but she would often be harassed by young males and sometimes the old "L" trains would simply not work. They never arrived or departed on time either.

Judy soon yearned to return to the flexibility and excitement of her career in journalism. Reporting gave her the ability to

40

Bureaucracy generally means the body of non-elected government officials that administers government. It is broken into departments staffed by non-elected officials, who help govern large institutions within governments at all levels: municipal, township, county, state, and federal. The term bureaucracy has developed a negative meaning today because it can often be too complex, inefficient, or inflexible.

41

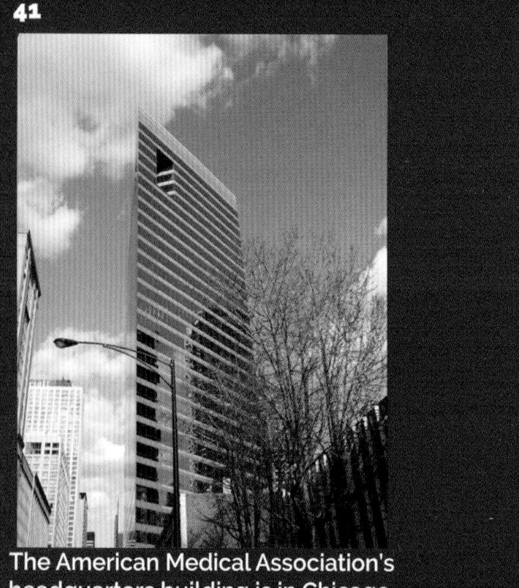

The American Medical Association's headquarters building is in Chicago.

move, think, write, and inform. She decided to start her own business in public relations, and began working out of her parents' real estate office in Berwyn. This created for Judy an incredible opportunity to work on her own while reaching out to the community in a very different manner. She also had the chance to make a living and contribute to the family income. It was yet again another career that was not traditionally pursued by women. Her public relations business brought her into close interactions with the community, just as journalism had done.

In public relations, Judy once again saw the same issues she had as a journalist, especially with regard to local government. She continued to be dismayed by the dysfunctional nature of local politics and eventually felt the need to do something about it. At some point during her stretch in public relations and while she was still writing part-time for newspapers like the *Forest Park Review*, the future Illinois treasurer, Illinois comptroller, and Illinois gubernatorial candidate had the idea to pursue a role in local government. It was a new idea for a woman in the community, and it was a decision that would lead her down a path in life that no one expected—including Judy herself—a political career in a state known for its crooked politics.

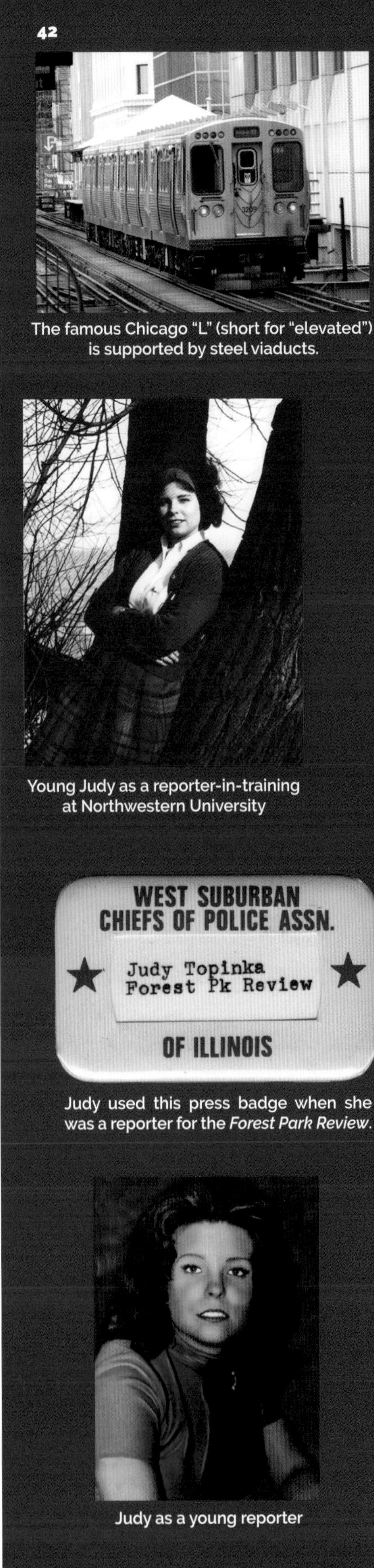

The famous Chicago "L" (short for "elevated") is supported by steel viaducts.

Young Judy as a reporter-in-training at Northwestern University

Judy used this press badge when she was a reporter for the *Forest Park Review*.

Judy as a young reporter

Resources for Further Research

These sites give your further background into the places where Judy worked:

- *Berwyn Life* (now part of a greater Suburban Life Newspapers system): http://www.mysuburbanlife.com/berwyn.
- *Forest Park Review*: http://www.forestparkreview.com.
- The American Medical Association (AMA): http://www.ama-assn.org/ama.
- Judy briefly owned her hometown newspaper, the *Riverside-Brookfield Landmark:* http://www.rblandmark.com/

To start learning more about local government, check out these sites:

- Township Officials of Illinois: https://www.toi.org/#events-tab.
- Illinois Municipal League provides a great amount of information on local governments: https://www.iml.org.
- Information about local, public access cable channels: http://www.accesschannel.com. These channels offer viewers the ability to watch local government bodies and the debate over local issues during public hearings.

And, to get out and about:

- Chicago Transit Authority (CTA): http://www.transitchicago.com.
- The Chicago Zoological Society's Brookfield Zoo: https://www.czs.org/Brookfield-ZOO/Home. Judy loved to visit this zoo and would visit it often with her family.

Civics Project Ideas and Classroom Learning Activities

- government institutions
- current and controversial issues
- service learning
- democratic processes
- heritage
-  compromise
-  leadership
-  critical thinking

Chapter 4 Key Concepts:

- Community Awareness and Involvement
- Mentorship
- Life Experience

Chapter 4 Classroom Activities (Teacher):

- Talk with students about their local communities and what different components comprise a community: schools and school systems, citizens, government and leadership, businesses...what else? Talk about how people can become involved in and support their community in lots of different ways, such as by volunteering, running for a local government office, joining the local school board, etc.
- GRADES 6–8: Define "mentor" for your students and ask students if they have any mentors? If so, who is that person and what is their relationship like? If not, how can they get a mentor?

Chapter 4 Essay Topics (Student):

- Visit your local police or fire station and ask its members about their role in the community. Write about what made them want to do what they are doing.
- GRADES 6–8: Read your local newspaper. Write an essay about an issue your local government is dealing with right now, and how you would handle it if you were in charge.

October 21, 2017

Dear Reader:

News reporters, good ones anyway, are not supposed to play favorites. However, anyone who followed political stories in Illinois would probably have noticed that Judy Baar Topinka seemed to be on television news programs or quoted in print and radio stories more than many others in politics. It was because she was accessible, articulate, and fueled by boundless energy. Journalists sought her out, because she usually had something profound—and quotable—to say. She knew what journalists needed to understand in order to write and balance their stories. That was no accident. As I learned when I started covering Judy in the Illinois General Assembly, she was an educated and experienced journalist herself.

I believe her early career is what made Judy Baar Topinka a different kind of politician and governmental leader. Finding a career as you get older is not always an easy task, and Judy's trek in becoming a journalist was fraught with obstacles due to her family's financial background and especially due to her being a woman.

Judy always seemed offended that there were people who did not always treat others equally based on things like race, sex, ethnicity, gender identity, or religion. As a journalist, Judy worked hard to overcome sexist attitudes through good writing and good investigative reporting. That is a lesson that we can all benefit from. Being very good at your work, or any task to which you are assigned, can often disarm those who think you are not up to the job.

I believe the decision to always strive for excellence made Judy Baar Topinka a great journalist as much as it made her a renowned legislator and constitutional officer. Judy did not take "no" for an answer, especially if she knew there were other answers to be found.

Judy Baar Topinka became a voice for women, for equality, and for bipartisanship in the General Assembly. Not that she wasn't partisan. She was a staunch Republican and was one of the GOP's most energetic cheerleaders, especially at political conventions. However, she was always true to her ideals, even when it went against the traditional party line. She did not win every political battle in her political career, but she certainly fought each and every one with energy, integrity, and conviction.

Judy was a politician and a leader. And, as we grew to know each other over the years, I also counted Judy as a friend. However, when it was time to do our respective jobs, we were all business.

I would often have Judy Baar Topinka as a guest on WBBM Radio's public affairs program, *At Issue*, (http://chicago.cbslocal.com/audio/at-issue/), and she would always deliver information and opinions with spirit, wit, wisdom, and simple, albeit blunt, honesty. You could always see the underpinnings of journalism in her. It was in her heart; it was her calling.

Among the lessons to be learned from Judy's life is that you should find a "calling" that you love and do not be afraid to change careers in life as Judy Baar Topinka did. As long as you love doing what you do, you will be happy and will contribute to your family and your community. Judy Baar Topinka knew she had great parents and a great education. And she knew those factors were key in helping her achieve many things in life.

Be like an investigative journalist, learn as much as you can, and never stop learning. There are so many great stories out there and so many great people to meet. You can learn so much from every one of them. My friend Judy's story was a great one. Learn from it and be inspired by it.

Sincerely,

Craig Dellimore

Craig Dellimore
Political Editor
WBBM Newsradio
Chicago, Illinois

43 The Burlington Northern railroad tracks were those that made Riverside such an opportune place to live as people could easily commute to Chicago every day. Today, those tracks are used by Metra, which operates the commuter trains around the Chicagoland area.

44 *Topinky* is Czech garlic toast, usually made of deep brown bread deep fried and served with raw garlic cloves.

45 Prague Castle (*Pražský hrad*) and the Charles Bridge over the Vltava River. The castle houses the Bohemian crown jewels.

46 Judy on her wedding day

The Personal Side

Just as in any fairytale, Judy Barbara Baar married her childhood sweetheart, Joe, and became Judy Baar Topinka. Her husband was four years older than she was and grew up on the other side of the railroad tracks in Riverside.[43] Topinka, which in Czech loosely means "garlic toast,"[44] is a more common name in the Czech Republic, especially around the capital city of Prague.[45] Even while Judy was away at high school in Lake Forest and Joe was in college out of state, the two stayed together despite the difficulties of communicating with each other. There were no cell phones, email, Skype, or social media in the 1950s and 1960s. It was difficult for them to talk to each other, making their relationship tough to maintain. When she was in high school, Judy often baked Joe cookies, then either sent them to him at college or delivered them in person if he was back home in Illinois. Long-distance romantic relationships are never easy, even today. Both Judy and Joe would have other boyfriends or girlfriends over the years, and there would be breakups, but they ultimately came together and married on June 20, 1964.[46]

Married life, however, was not the "happily ever after" that Judy envisioned. It was a lot of work for her, and she found it challenging to be a traditional wife staying home to cook, clean, and take care of a child. She often declared that she was no "Suzy Homemaker." Such responsibilities were alien to Judy, who never really experienced them growing up as her grandmother and mother did the cooking and cleaning. She and her husband had not really planned for what married life would be like for the long term. Marriage was considered customary for all in the mid-twentieth century, but neither of these two were ready for what it entailed. They hadn't even completed their education when they wed. Years later, Judy told her son that love was wonderful, but it alone didn't put the food on the table, and that a husband and wife needed to work together to earn livings, and to be partners. "A strong friendship was the best foundation for marriage," she advised. Judy always felt in retrospect that she married too young and should have joined the military instead. The military was not a popular track for women in the 1960s. Women did not have the same opportunities that men had until later in the century and after a great debate in the country over the Equal Rights Amendment to the U.S. Constitution.[47] College, journalism, joining the military—such opportunities and many more were either not open or not typical for women back then. Judy and other women lived through these times and did not like it. Judy tried her best to make opportunities happen then and for the rest of her life even if it meant upsetting others, especially men. In looking back, Judy believed she would have been a better fit for the U.S. Navy than for a traditional marriage and housekeeping duties.[48]

Despite her ambivalence about the traditional married lifestyle, according to Judy, "her greatest accomplishment was the birth and raising of her son." She and Joe named him Joseph after his father, his grandfather, and his great-grandfather. With so many Joes in the family, Judy gave her son the nickname of "Pepi," which loosely translates to Joe in Czech. Like her parents before her, she depended on her parents to help take care of Pepi while he was growing up. Both she and her husband worked full-time, just as so many people have to do today.

During this era—the early 1970s—most women still stayed home in a more old-fashioned manner to take care of the house and children. Not Judy, though. She did try to do traditional mom duties like being a Cub Scout den mother[49] and cooking. She also ensured that her son went to Czech school, took piano lessons, and participated in Moravian[50] dancing. Joseph would learn about his Czech heritage and the importance of music. But Judy was just not good at being a stay-at-home parent.

Take, for example, the time Judy made a chocolate cake with too many chocolate chips in the batter. The chips melted when the cake baked. After frosting the cake right after it came out of the oven, she put the cake in the freezer without waiting for it to cool (mistake!). When she then took the cake

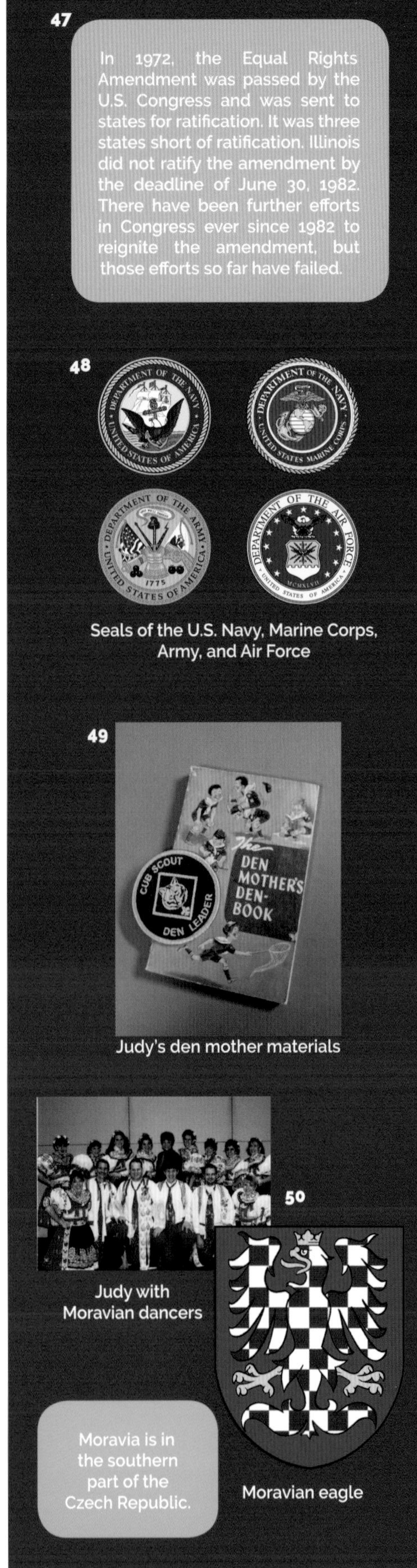

47 In 1972, the Equal Rights Amendment was passed by the U.S. Congress and was sent to states for ratification. It was three states short of ratification. Illinois did not ratify the amendment by the deadline of June 30, 1982. There have been further efforts in Congress ever since 1982 to reignite the amendment, but those efforts so far have failed.

48 Seals of the U.S. Navy, Marine Corps, Army, and Air Force

49 Judy's den mother materials

50 Judy with Moravian dancers

Moravian eagle

Moravia is in the southern part of the Czech Republic.

Record of Birth

This certifies that

FAMILY HISTORY

Pepi's birth certificate

Judy and Pepi in 1969

The official family photo for Judy's first campaign for state representative

to her newspaper job for a friend's birthday, no one could cut the cake because the excess chocolate in the cake had frozen solid. She would be known from that point on as the maker of "brick" or "concrete" cakes.

When microwave ovens first came out, the family purchased one. One morning, Judy tried to make her son eggs in the new appliance. They blew up. She figured there was something wrong with the eggs so she cleaned up the oven and tried again. The same thing happened—again and again. Finally, Judy and Pepi could only laugh. It was very funny and Judy conjectured that microwave ovens must be very different from normal ovens. The kitchen was not her place, and neither was the laundry room. Judy was known to use wrong detergents and water temperatures, causing clothes to turn different colors. In other words, pink underwear and socks were commonplace in the Topinka household.

While there were mishaps at home, Judy excelled at taking her son "on safari" around Chicagoland. She took Pepi on tours of the city's many neighborhoods, showing him how a trip to an ethnic neighborhood could be like traveling to another country, only cheaper. Through the then Chicago Council on Foreign Relations, she took him to Mexican, Ukrainian, Chinese, Korean, and Polish neighborhoods, just to name only a few. She also took him to Chicago's incredible museums and the historic locations that made Chicago the once great, industrial center of the world. From Stephen Douglas's tomb on the South Side to the location of the St. Valentine's Day Massacre on the North Side, Judy's son learned about the historic good, bad, and ugly of Chicago as well as its surrounding communities. Every weekend was a mom-and-son adventure in history even though they often got lost on the way. Judy was a horrible driver and Pepi was an equally poor navigator.

Judy and her husband, Joe, divorced in 1979, about the same time she began her political career. It was hard to balance a family life with a career in elected office. Both partners realized they wanted something different out of life, and the two grew apart in many ways during their 16-year marriage. Divorce was a more complicated process in the 1970s, requiring many legalities that put everyone through great stress, especially Judy's young son. Paying the legal fees for the antiquated divorce process in Illinois in that era left both Judy and her former husband close to financial ruin, and their parents had to help both of them out so that they could move forward. Later, based on her experience, Judy would support no-fault divorce laws as a state representative to make the process easier and less emotional and traumatic for Illinois families.

Like so many parents today, Judy and her ex-husband decided to share joint custody of their son, but joint custody can be very much like being a single parent. Judy never forgot that experience and her awareness of the challenges facing single mothers. There were late nights on the floor of the Illinois House of Representatives when she called her son from under her (tiny!) desk so reporters couldn't see her and so she could have some level of privacy. The floor of the Illinois House of Representatives could be very noisy, especially back then, when there were 177 members (today there are only 118).[51] It was also not easy raising a child when her ex-husband had one set of ideas about parenting and she had another. These are common experiences among all parents who divorce. They both love their children tremendously, but they may have different ideas about parenting. Judy's experiences as a parent raising a child under joint custody would forever influence her views on divorce, custody, and the emotional consequences to children of divorce as a government official.

Judy had some very specific passions and hobbies. She loved learning about and experiencing all religions, but she was raised Roman Catholic and enjoyed the Catholic culture even though she disagreed with some of the Church's teachings. Despite having limited funds for luxuries, Judy loved to see the world, especially with her son, and they traveled widely. She also loved to read, particularly histories and biographies. She enjoyed estate sales and developed a reputation for finding great deals on items from all over the state of Illinois. Finally, Judy loved animals and hated to see or hear about their mistreatment.

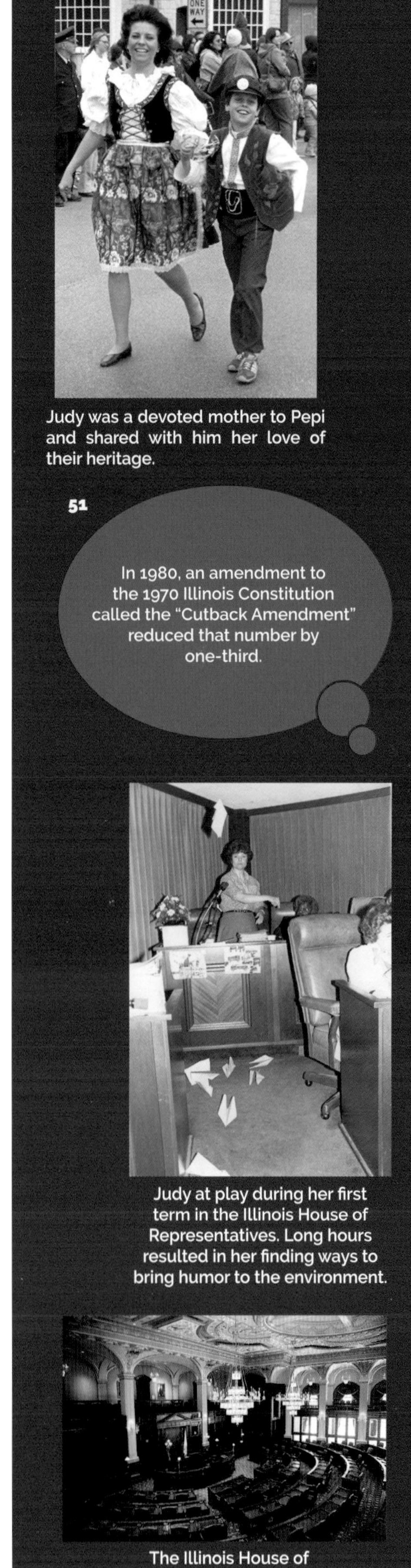

Judy was a devoted mother to Pepi and shared with him her love of their heritage.

51 In 1980, an amendment to the 1970 Illinois Constitution called the "Cutback Amendment" reduced that number by one-third.

Judy at play during her first term in the Illinois House of Representatives. Long hours resulted in her finding ways to bring humor to the environment.

The Illinois House of Representatives chamber

52, 53

Symbols of the Holy See, the seat of the Catholic Church, and the Society of Jesus (Jesuits)

54

British Houses of Parliament on the Thames River in London

55

Westminster Abbey is normally where kings and queens of the United Kingdom are coronated, and it is the burial site for past monarchs and noteworthy British poets, authors, scientists, and other national figures.

56

After World War II and a 1948 coup, Czechoslovakia was ruled by a Communist government affiliated with the former Soviet Union. This government ruled from 1948 to 1989 in a totalitarian manner. All aspects of lives were controlled by the government and dominated by the Soviet Union and an ideology based on Marxism and Leninism.

The beauty and majesty of the Catholic Church were so important to Judy.[52] She preferred the Jesuit philosophies within the Church because the Jesuit order[53] encouraged teaching. Learning was a never-ending pursuit for Judy. She admired other religions as much as she admired other cultures. Judy visited churches, synagogues, mosques, temples, and just about any place of worship when she travelled around Illinois, the United States, and the rest of the world.

While Judy loved reading, she found traveling to be the greatest form of education since it was three-dimensional and immersive. It involved sight, sound, taste, and touch. When a person travels, he or she can meet other people and see how they live in a way that no book can ever replicate. Traveling also allows people to see the artifacts of history. Judy once visited the British House of Commons[54] with her son and simply couldn't leave because it was so interesting to watch the debate process in person. It was nothing like what she did in the Illinois House of Representatives or the Illinois Senate. She loved to visit Westminster Abbey[55] in London and the feeling it provided of being close to so many great leaders, poets, writers, and scientists in one spot. These were places where she could connect with the past. She very much enjoyed visiting the Czech Republic to research her family background. Her family in the Czech Republic was always quite dear to her. She would always worry about family members when they lived in the former Czechoslovakia[56] under Communist rule from the 1940s until the late 1980s. She was so happy when the oppressive Communist rule disappeared during what is known today as the Velvet Revolution.[57] Judy wrote to her family often, packed food for them every year during the holidays, and even sent money orders to them when necessary until her death.

Reading was so very important to Judy. She read almost every major newspaper printed in Illinois nearly every day, often reading well past midnight. She believed that only through reading articles from different perspectives could a person truly develop their own perspective on the issues of the day.

She also read about her favorite leaders, Elizabeth I, Napoleon, and Joan of Arc. She believed that other people's lives taught critical lessons for later generations to follow. Elizabeth saw in her country, England, the foundation for an empire, and she pursued it with courage and zeal. Her efforts led to the formation of the British Empire that would influence the world, especially the United States, for centuries. Napoleon saw the vacuum of power left after the French Revolution and filled it with his energy, organization, and inspiration to create the most powerful country in nineteenth-century Europe. Judy saw such greatness in these leaders, and she envisioned a similar greatness for her country, her state, and its citizens. Her reading of biographies may have made her a bit idealistic,[58] but she was comfortable with being idealistic.

While traveling around Illinois, especially when she was running for state-wide office, Judy developed a love for going to estate sales.[59] She loved the hunt for items of interest, especially antiques and items of historical interest. And, she loved a bargain. She would negotiate for longer than you'd think possible to get the lowest price on something she wanted. In her daily life, she generally preferred to shop at Goodwill stores, Salvation Army stores, and consignment shops for what she needed. This matched how she would conduct herself in government, always trying to save money for the State of Illinois. She basically did not like any kind of waste, whether in her personal life or in the public arena.

Judy's greatest enthusiasm was her love of animals, something she carried over from the days of her pet bunny. She especially loved dogs. Her first dog was named Houby (sounds like ho-bee), which is Czech for mushroom. Houby was a huge Norwegian Elkhound she loved with all her heart.[60] When Houby was nearing the end of his life, she took him to the veterinarian. There, she stayed with him and held his paw while he died in front of her. She had many other dogs after Houby, including Greta, Romeo, Molly, and Andy, and she loved them with all her heart for their very short lives. And she held each one's paw as they died. Many of them were

57 People protested all over Czechoslovakia from November 17 to December 29, 1989. On November 28, the Communist Party announced that it would give up its power and take apart the one-party state of Czechoslovakia. Two days later, the legislature took out the sections in the Czechoslovakian Constitution that gave the Communists a monopoly of power. Shortly after, barbed wire and other fortifications were removed from the borders with West Germany and Austria, which Judy and her son had seen when visiting Czechoslovakia in 1978. On December 10, President Gustáv Husák appointed the first largely non-communist government in Czechoslovakia since 1948 and resigned. Alexander Dubček was elected speaker of parliament on December 28 and Václav Havel the president of Czechoslovakia on December 29, 1989. In June 1990, Czechoslovakia held its first free election since 1946.

Above, Tomáš Masaryk and Václav Havel, the first and tenth presidents of Czechoslovakia. Havel was later elected the first president of the Czech Republic. To the right, Joan of Arc

58 Idealism has many meanings but in Judy's life, it was her attitude of wanting to strive for some higher standard of behavior and honesty regarding government management. It was almost like a philosophy of how to run government for the good of the people in an environment of Illinois politics where often people do not have the best interest of the citizens at heart.

59 Estate sales are like garage sales but often involve the entire contents of someone's home or estate, after they have died. At these sales, people can purchase expensive items for very low prices.

what she would term "pound dogs" because she would find them in animal shelters in suburban Chicago or Springfield or through Scottie Rescue. She often referred to her animals as "chudáks" (sounds like hood-aak) which in Czech loosely means a poor or sad creature. She donated money to animal charities constantly and ultimately developed a program in the Illinois Treasurer's Office called *Treasured Pets* and one in the Illinois Comptroller's Office called *Comptroller's Critters*[61] focusing on finding homes for abandoned animals.

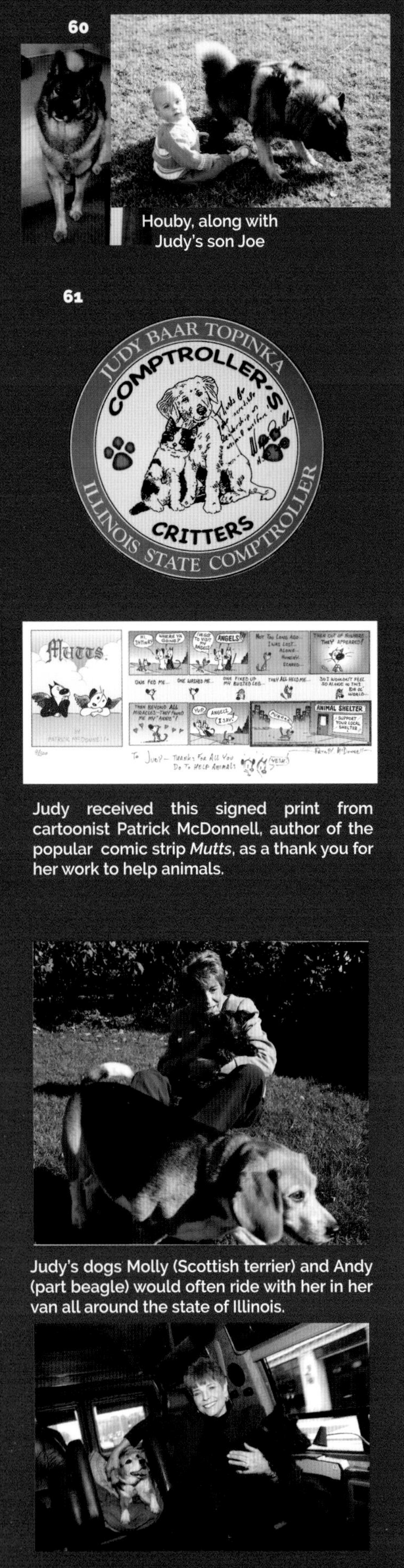

Houby, along with Judy's son Joe

Judy received this signed print from cartoonist Patrick McDonnell, author of the popular comic strip *Mutts*, as a thank you for her work to help animals.

Judy's dogs Molly (Scottish terrier) and Andy (part beagle) would often ride with her in her van all around the state of Illinois.

Resources for Further Research

Metra (http://metrarail.com/metra/wap/en/home.html) is the commuter train service that operates around the Chicagoland area. Riverside can be reached on the Burlington Northern Metra line.

The City of Prague (http://www.prague.eu/en) is the capital of the Czech Republic.

Moravia (http://www.czechtourism.com/a/moravia-silesia) is a historic Czech region. The United Moravian Societies (http://unitedmoraviansocieties.org) has a great wealth of information about Moravia and sponsors an annual Moravian Festival outside Chicago.

The Boy Scouts of America (http://www.scouting.org) are divided into various local councils. Judy was a den mother with the Des Plaines Valley Council, a former scouting council that was headquartered in La Grange, Illinois, until 2014, when it merged with other local Illinois councils.

The official website of the Holy See is at http://w2.vatican.va/content/vatican/en.html. The Archdiocese of Chicago is located at http://www.archdioceseofchicago.org.

Two of Judy's favorite places to visit were the British Parliament (https://www.parliament.uk) and Westminster Abbey (http://www.westminster-abbey.org), both in London. Judy admired Elizabeth I and Napoleon Bonaparte. The history channel provides a summary of Elizabeth's life (http://www.history.co.uk/biographies/queen-elizabeth-i). Elizabeth I is buried in Westminster Abbey. The Napoleonic Historical Society (http://www.napoleonichistoricalsociety.org) is located in Chicago near O'Hare International Airport. Napoleon is entombed in the Royal Chapel at Les Invalides in Paris (http://www.musee-armee.fr/en/collections/museum-spaces/dome-des-invalides-tomb-of-napoleon-i.html).

Judy donated money and time to many charities for animals, especially those that supported no-kill policies. One of her favorite organizations in Illinois was PAWS (http://www.pawschicago.org). The Illinois Comptroller's Office still sponsors Comptroller's Critters (http://illinoiscomptroller.gov/services/critters), an animal adoption program Judy started while in office.

The Equal Rights Amendment has been a source of great debate for many years. Judy supported the amendment. More information about the Amendment is at http://www.equalrightsamendment.org.

The Chicago Council on Foreign Relations is now called the Chicago Forum on Global Affairs. Information on its activities is located at https://www.thechicagocouncil.org/events.

Civics Project Ideas and Classroom Learning Activities

government institutions
current and controversial issues
service learning
democratic processes
heritage
compromise
leadership
critical thinking

Chapter 5 Key Concepts:

- Family
- Marriage
- Divorce
- Travel
- Reading
- Animals

Chapter 5 Classroom Activities (Teacher):

- Ask students about where they most want to travel and why.
- Invite students to stand up and talk about their favorite book and why they like it.
- In small groups, have students discuss the importance of family in their lives.

Chapter 5 Essay Topics (Student):

- Choose a book and read it. Write why you chose the book and whether you enjoyed reading the book. How do you think it may influence you in your life now and later?
- Did you ever have a pet or did you ever go to the zoo? What is your favorite animal? Write about that animal or a favorite pet describing why that animal is so important to you.
- Have you traveled anywhere in your home state? If so, where have you gone and why? If not, where would you want to visit?
- Have you ever made a family tree? Judy Baar Topinka loved to make family trees. Try making one for your family by talking to your family members about your ancestors. How far back can you go?

Making Laws!

On July 31, 1979, Judy Baar Topinka announced she was running for state representative in the 7th District of Illinois. She made the announcement at the Old Prague Restaurant in Berwyn, Illinois, as she wanted to announce her candidacy in a place that represented her Czech and Slovak heritage. Her whole family was there, including her parents, her husband, and her son. She told the crowd that "somewhere along the line, our faith in ourselves began to crumble. We became economically stagnant. Progress became non-existent. Our sense of community and duty to ourselves and our children has been replaced by irresponsibility and lack of will. Pride has given way to a lack of confidence in our system. Leadership no longer exists." [62]

Judy—people everywhere were used to calling her by her first name from her reporter days—had first tried to get involved in local government before she ever considered running for state office. She wanted a position in Riverside Township where she lived. What she learned covering municipal governments as a reporter for so many years had made her angry. She was frustrated by all the ways local leaders were not properly managing or serving their communities, and she saw such things as favors for special people or companies, the promotion of higher taxes for fewer services, and the creation of burdensome local rules. To top it off, when she had approached village and township political leaders, they had found her interest in public office quaint, dismissing her with words to the effect of *stay at home and take care of your child*. Judy disliked being told what she couldn't do, and she really resented being treated differently because she was a woman.

But then a seat opened up in the 7th Legislative District. With her interest in municipal-level politics, it was an opening that Judy hadn't even considered until her mother encouraged her to go for it. Judy wasn't the only person who wanted the position. She lived in a mostly Republican area, but she could have easily run as a Democrat.[63] Both parties had characteristics that she admired and those that she disliked. She chose to be a Republican and

CITIZENS TO ELECT
JUDY BAAR TOPINKA
7th DISTRICT REPRESENTATIVE
6335 WEST CERMAK ROAD BERWYN, ILLINOIS 60402 TELEPHONE 795-8266

FOR RELEASE AFTER JULY 31, 1979

TOPINKA ANNOUNCES CANDIDACY

Judy Baar Topinka today (July 31) announced her candidacy for state representative, 7th District, in the March, 1980 Republican primary election.

The announcement was made during a press conference held at Old Prague Restaurant, 6928 West Cermak Road, Cicero, Illinois, which was attended by her family, committee and supporters.

"I believe I can provide the confident, practical leadership that will work in the ... of the people of this district...es... these times when lack of direction ... drift are the rule rather than the ... said.

A life-long Republican, she ... been active in community, business, ... ethnic and political organizations ... She lives in Riverside with her hu... Topinka, vice president and genera... Equipment Company, LaGrange, and h... Joseph Baar Topinka (Pepi), a stat... Riverside's Hauser Junior High Sch... are William and Lillian Baar of Ri... Baar and Baar Realtors, Berwyn.

It was during her many years ...

(more)
"Leadership that Works"

62

CITIZENS TO ELECT
JUDY BAAR TOPINKA
7th DISTRICT REPRESENTATIVE
6335 WEST CERMAK ROAD BERWYN, ILLINOIS 60402 TELEPHONE 795-8266

FOR IMMEDIATE RELEASE

TOPINKA CITES 'LEADERSHIP THAT WORKS' AS THEME TO PRIMARY ELECTION CAMPAIGN

"The theme of my campaign will be 'Leadership that Works,' said Judy Baar Topinka as she announced her candidacy for state representative, 7th District, in the March, 1980 Republican primary election.

"I think that this theme sets the tone and the pace for the residents of the 7th legislative district to understand my thinking and my style of getting things done.

"It is a theme that focuses upon three very broad but important qualities that I want everyone to know about me. First, that I am a leader; second, that I am a hard worker in everything that I undertake; and third, and perhaps most importantly, that I can provide the confident, practical leadership that will work in the best interests of the people of this district.

"As I look around me, I see that the communities of the 7th district have lost their once positive momentum. Somewhere along the line our faith in ourselves and in what we could achieve began to crumble. We have become economically stagnant. Progress is non-existent. Our sense of community and duty to ourselves and to our children has been replaced by

(more) "Leadership that Works"

The press release announcing Judy's candidacy

The United States is divided primarily into two major parties, Republican and Democratic. The Republican party (represented by an elephant) has a reputation of favoring smaller government and more conservative perspectives. The Democratic party (represented by a donkey) advocates more government intervention and more liberal perspectives. Some much smaller parties exist in the United States such as the Green Party and the Libertarian Party. Some people are not affiliated with a party. They are called Independents.

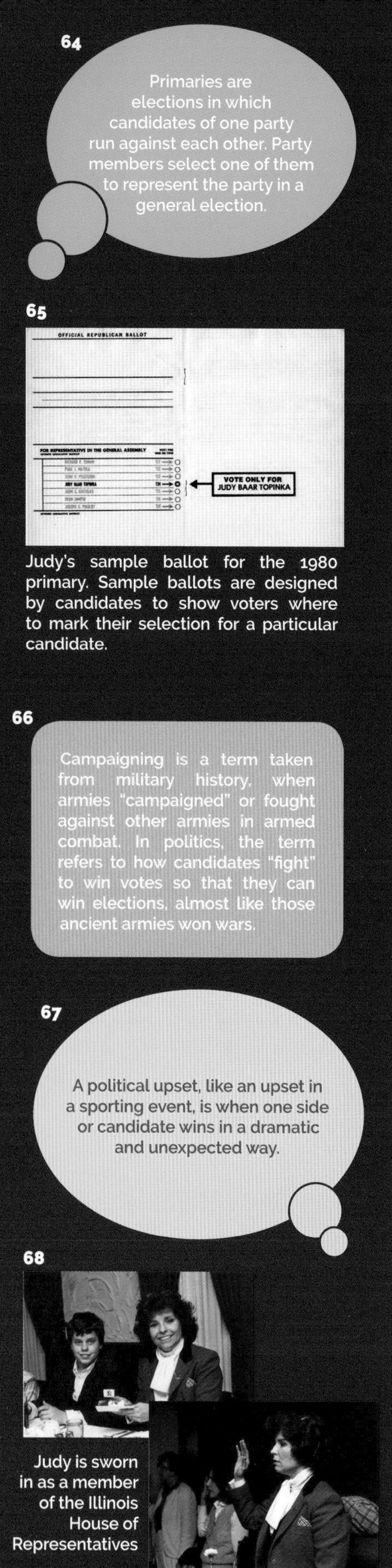

64 Primaries are elections in which candidates of one party run against each other. Party members select one of them to represent the party in a general election.

65 Judy's sample ballot for the 1980 primary. Sample ballots are designed by candidates to show voters where to mark their selection for a particular candidate.

66 Campaigning is a term taken from military history, when armies "campaigned" or fought against other armies in armed combat. In politics, the term refers to how candidates "fight" to win votes so that they can win elections, almost like those ancient armies won wars.

67 A political upset, like an upset in a sporting event, is when one side or candidate wins in a dramatic and unexpected way.

68 Judy is sworn in as a member of the Illinois House of Representatives

run as a Republican because it would be her best chance to win in the general election in November 1980. But first she had to win a Republican primary,[64] against six men.[65]

Many people dismissed Judy's candidacy and most of those people were men. Some actually laughed at her—even in public. It was a trying time, and Judy worked very hard by going door-to-door and talking to people all over the district, which included the Town of Cicero, the City of Berwyn, part of the Village of Lyons, and part of the Village of Brookfield. She didn't know how to run a campaign and had to create a committee of friends and supporters who knew how to organize, market, and help Judy develop a winning strategy to help her win the Republican primary and then the general election. She also had to start a political campaign fund under state law. Political campaigns cost a lot of money to run, and Judy was not independently wealthy, so she needed to ask people to donate to her campaign fund. When donations started coming in for that fund, Judy had not even opened a bank account for that purpose. A quickly thought-up solution was to put donated cash into the family freezer until one was established. In the meantime, the Topinka family had a lot of "cool cash" at its home on Selborne Road in Riverside.

Running for office was intimidating to Judy and time-consuming. Judy didn't see her husband or son very much while campaigning[66] because she had to attend meetings, meet people at events, get interviewed by journalists, and ask for donations for her campaign fund. When she did see her family, it was often when they were together as a family at a political event. Even Joe's 12th birthday celebration in February 1980 was at a political event in a banquet hall in Lombard, Illinois. The pressures of that first run for office on her family, and Judy herself, were intense, but even in the face of great odds, Judy never gave up. Her tough uphill battled culminated on March 18, 1980, the day of the Republican primary and a political "upset."[67] Many people were surprised—including Judy—and her family was very proud. Judy Baar Topinka had won her first election.

The strain of Judy's entry into the political sphere, however, had taken its toll on her marriage, and it would be over several months later. Yet the important campaign was still ahead for the seat in the general election in November 1980. Judy Baar Topinka won the general election and her first public office!

In January 1981, Judy, her son, Joe, and some of their friends traveled to Springfield, Illinois, where she was sworn in as an Illinois state representative.[68] She really didn't know what to expect in the General Assembly,[69] the formal name for the legislative body of Illinois government. (Congress is the legislative branch of our federal government in Washington, D.C.) She was surrounded by men, many of whom had been legislators in Illinois for years. Because the floor of the Illinois House of Representatives was so crowded, her family had to watch Judy from a remote camera in another part of the state capitol after she was sworn in. Later that day, Judy was asked to be the first person to nominate a Republican legislator from Kankakee, Illinois, to be the next Speaker of the House.[70] His name was George Ryan,[71] and he would be a familiar figure in Illinois government for many years to come. Judy told Joe that it was a great honor to be the first person to nominate Ryan for the highest office in the Illinois House.

Otherwise, Judy was like anyone else in a new job: she really didn't know what to do and she needed to learn fast. Something she found odd was the very small bathroom for female legislators, and she noted that the few women serving in the House often had to leave the floor to use public restrooms in other parts of the capitol building. Years later, she encountered a similar inadequate and unequal bathroom situation in the other chamber of the Illinois General Assembly, the Senate.

In the weeks and months that followed that cold day in January 1981, Judy learned about the legislative process, sharing with Joe what she learned.[72] Her young son would say: "It is just like in the cartoon from *Schoolhouse Rock!* where the bill becomes a law!"[73] She would recall her days as a rookie legislator as some of the hardest of her life—learning the ropes of being

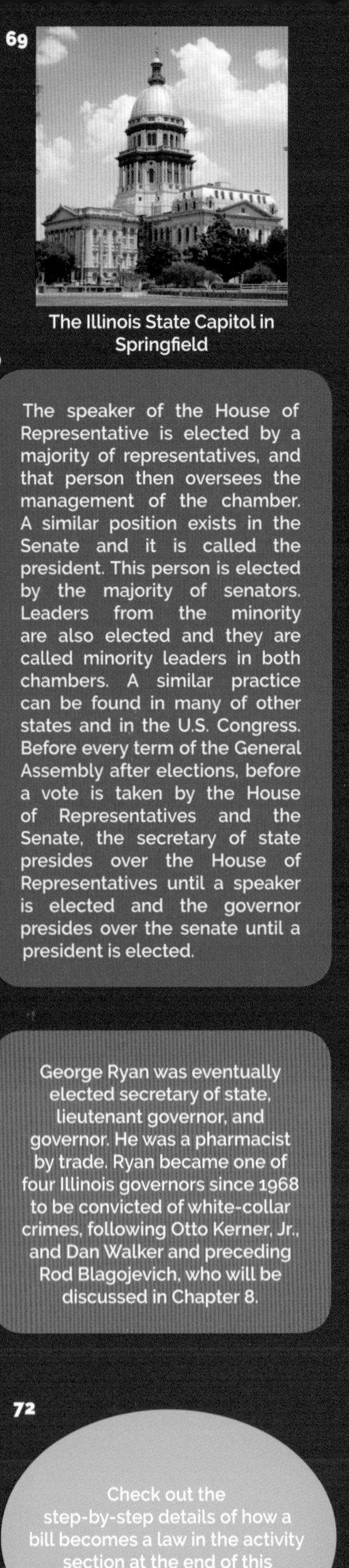

69

The Illinois State Capitol in Springfield

70

The speaker of the House of Representative is elected by a majority of representatives, and that person then oversees the management of the chamber. A similar position exists in the Senate and it is called the president. This person is elected by the majority of senators. Leaders from the minority are also elected and they are called minority leaders in both chambers. A similar practice can be found in many of other states and in the U.S. Congress. Before every term of the General Assembly after elections, before a vote is taken by the House of Representatives and the Senate, the secretary of state presides over the House of Representatives until a speaker is elected and the governor presides over the senate until a president is elected.

71

George Ryan was eventually elected secretary of state, lieutenant governor, and governor. He was a pharmacist by trade. Ryan became one of four Illinois governors since 1968 to be convicted of white-collar crimes, following Otto Kerner, Jr., and Dan Walker and preceding Rod Blagojevich, who will be discussed in Chapter 8.

72

Check out the step-by-step details of how a bill becomes a law in the activity section at the end of this chapter.

a lawmaker[74] while at the same time parenting a son through the push and pull of a divorce.

Like many outsiders participating in the process for the first time, Judy found her pet peeves. One thing that truly irritated her was when fellow legislators would push the "present" button during a vote on something substantial like a bill, amendment, or resolution. On the floors of both the House of Representatives and the Senate, legislators choose among three buttons during a vote: green (to vote "aye," meaning *yes*), red (to vote "nay," meaning *no*), or yellow (to vote "present").[75] What did that mean? Judy told her son over and over that a "yellow vote is a no vote," and a legislator who could not vote *aye* or *nay* on an issue should not be a legislator in Springfield.

Another thing that annoyed Judy was how late into the night members of both chambers would meet when the end of the legislative session was nearing and budget bills needed to be passed. She resented that the four legislative leaders (House speaker, House minority leader, Senate president, and Senate minority leader) would meet with the governor and come up with a "deal," and then the legislators would have to vote on the deal without even having a chance to read it, or else a budget would not get passed. In other words, a small group, usually of men, made a compromise, and that compromise "was rammed down the throats of all the legislators." If the legislators did not vote on the compromise, they could not get home by the July 4th holiday to march in parades and see their constituents and families. At least one year, Judy and her colleagues did not get home by the 4th because a compromise came too late. That year, Judy's son was serving as a page in the Illinois House of Representatives. Both of them returned home from Springfield seeing fireworks along the way. That was the only year Judy ever missed marching in a 4th of July parade with her fellow citizens.

The vital thing Judy learned in her first two-year term as a state representative was that compromise and collegiality were key in getting bills passed and laws made. It did not matter if you were a Republican or Democrat, you had to work together with

73 *Schoolhouse Rock!* was a popular cartoon in the 1970s that taught children many different subjects through animation and music.

74

43RD LEGISLATIVE DISTRICT

REP. JUDY BAAR TOPINKA GETS THE TOUGH JOBS DONE

In her first term in Springfield Rep. Judy Baar Topinka, got the job done for the people in her district.

Judy initiated the legislation and secured the funding for the badly needed Ogden Avenue Sewer Project. The $3 million public improvement is underway.

Rep. Topinka's leadership resulted in the establishment of local senior citizen programs, she's working to restore the historic Hoffman Tower in Lyons and the relocation and restoration of a famous Czech landmark in Chicago.

Judy is the only freshman Representative named to four major House Committees, two State Commissions, and a Federal Commission.

Her top priority is keeping in close contact with the people with full time service offices in the District and Springfield.

Gov. Jim Thompson said "Rep. Topinka is an articulate, effective, energetic young leader in the Illinois General Assembly."

A lifelong resident of the area, Judy is active in her community. She is a Northwestern University graduate.

75

Voting buttons at a legislator's desk

In our opinion

Democracy at best

Never let it be said that politicians won't respond to their constituents.

The culmination of the long drive to secure partial state funding for repairs to the rotting sewer which runs under Ogden on Brookfield's east side is testimony to the premise that public pressure can do some good.

A lot of people deserve pats on the back for the Ogden sewer funding effort.

But at the forefront should be State Rep. Judy Baar Topinka (R-7th) who spearheaded the drive to push legislation through Springfield and past Governor Thompson with a vengeance like the state capital has never seen before.

Long before she was even elected last November, Topinka promised she'd push hard for legislation to fund sewer repairs along Ogden.

Unlike many politicians, Topinka made good on her promise, showing tremendous leadership and legislative skill in steering the legislation through the House and Senate.

Together with her staff, Topinka did an unbelievable job in gathering up the forces to put pressure on a reluctant Governor Thompson.

Those forces showed that an organized campaign of letter writing, phone calls, petitions and newspaper coverage can call attention to a local problem which needs the immediate attention of the state or federal government.

The Suburban LIFE Citizen is proud to have been an integral part of such a campaign from the beginning and we were happy to welcome our competitors and Chicago news media aboard the effort when they joined in once the campaign hit full steam.

The legislators from the 6th and 7th Districts played an integral role behind the scenes in Springfield. Sen. Mark Rhoads (R-6th) laid the groundwork in the legislature a year ago and Sen. Leonard Becker (R-7th) used his expertise to help guide the legislation through his chamber this summer.

And finally the ultimate credit must go to Governor James Thompson, a man who has been under tremendous pressure in the last four months.

Despite major troubles in state transportation, budgets and school systems, Thompson found time to investigate the Ogden sewer's problems. He even set aside several hours for a late spring visit to the scene.

He didn't have to sign the sewer bills. In fact, his budget director and several other aides didn't want him to.

But the Governor had the courage and the conviction to buck his so-called experts' opinion and sign the

This article showed that Judy always did her best to keep her promises, a characteristic of hers that people loved.

other lawmakers on behalf of your constituents—the voters of your district and the voters of the state—for the common interest, the public good. In other words, she recognized that a big part of her job was to get along with others, whatever their party affiliation and whatever their position in the legislative or executive branches. It was this insight and attitude that helped Judy work with members of both chambers as well as the governor to pass probably the biggest bill of her days as a state representative, the reconstruction of the massive sewer under Ogden Avenue in the municipalities of Brookfield and LaGrange, Illinois.[76] Her efforts ensured that critical infrastructure in her district survived, and she proved to her voters that she kept her promises.[77]

After her first term as a state representative, Judy ran for another two-year term. When cumulative voting in Illinois ended in 1982, Judy ran in the 43rd Legislative District race and won that election. Her new district was now one of two legislative districts in the 22nd Senatorial District. The overall Illinois House of Representatives was reduced in size by one-third as a result of the "Cutback Amendment." From 1870 to 1980, cumulative voting was used to elect members of the House of Representatives. In 1980, the amendment to the Illinois Constitution reduced the size of the House by one-third in order to reduce the costs of conducting legislative sessions. Judy saw many of her colleagues either lose elections or simply leave after this reduction was implemented through the amendment. It was an important lesson to learn: In politics, nothing is permanent. Colleagues come and go.

The Illinois House of Representatives was now lead by a different speaker. His name was Michael Madigan, and he was a Democrat from Chicago. Judy respected Speaker Madigan because he ran the House very efficiently, but she also realized that he was a cold, calculating, and shrewd politician. Her art of compromise would be forever honed by working with Madigan, and Judy acquired lots of political savvy from the experience. Madigan, along with George Ryan, were role models for Judy; both had admirable characteristics that she

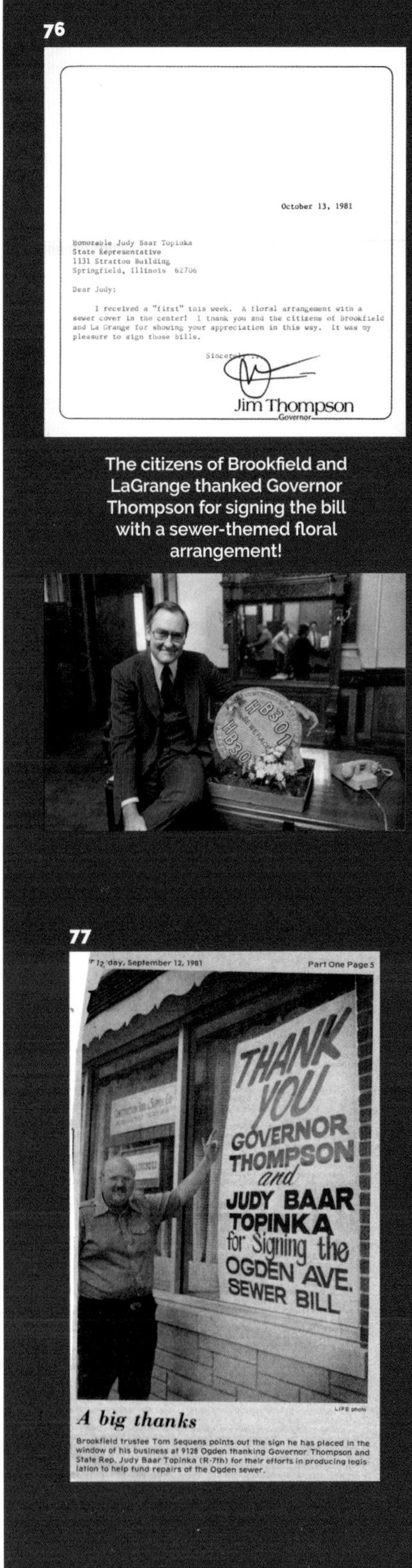

76

October 13, 1981

Honorable Judy Baar Topinka
State Representative
1131 Stratton Building
Springfield, Illinois 62706

Dear Judy:

I received a "first" this week. A floral arrangement with a sewer cover in the center! I thank you and the citizens of Brookfield and La Grange for showing your appreciation in this way. It was my pleasure to sign those bills.

Sincerely,

Jim Thompson
Governor

The citizens of Brookfield and LaGrange thanked Governor Thompson for signing the bill with a sewer-themed floral arrangement!

77

day, September 12, 1981 Part One Page 5

LIFE photo

A big thanks

Brookfield trustee Tom Sequens points out the sign he has placed in the window of his business at 9128 Ogden thanking Governor Thompson and State Rep. Judy Baar Topinka (R-7th) for their efforts in producing legislation to help fund repairs of the Ogden sewer.

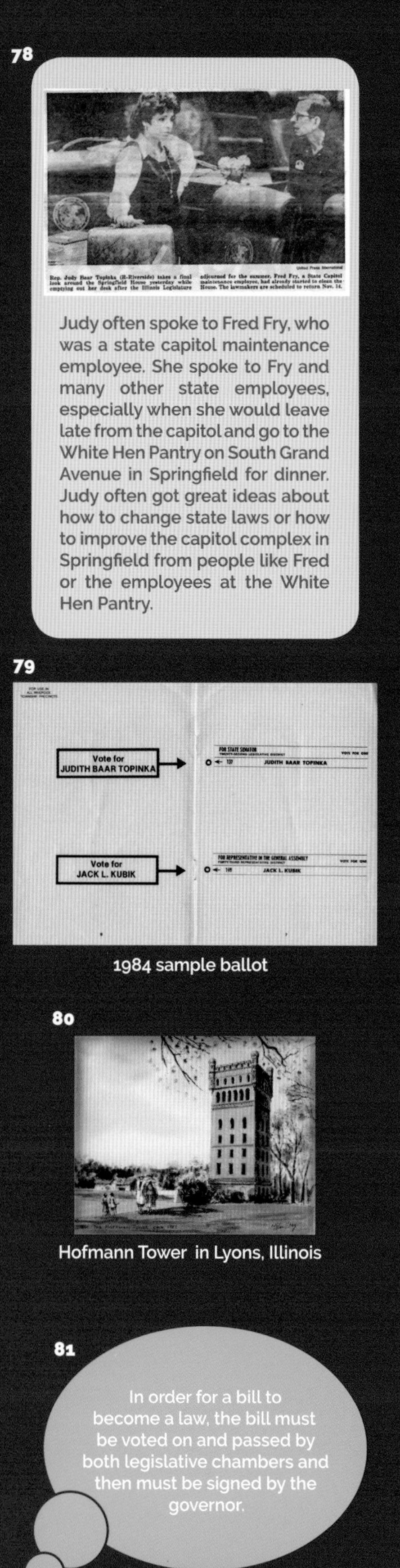

78

United Press International

Rep. Judy Baar Topinka (R-Riverside) takes a final look around the Springfield House yesterday while emptying out her desk after the Illinois Legislature adjourned for the summer. Fred Fry, a State Capitol maintenance employee, had already started to clean the House. The lawmakers are scheduled to return Nov. 14.

Judy often spoke to Fred Fry, who was a state capitol maintenance employee. She spoke to Fry and many other state employees, especially when she would leave late from the capitol and go to the White Hen Pantry on South Grand Avenue in Springfield for dinner. Judy often got great ideas about how to change state laws or how to improve the capitol complex in Springfield from people like Fred or the employees at the White Hen Pantry.

79

1984 sample ballot

80

Hofmann Tower in Lyons, Illinois

81

In order for a bill to become a law, the bill must be voted on and passed by both legislative chambers and then must be signed by the governor.

endeavored to emulate. However, both also had qualities that she actively dismissed and avoided. Judy made a point of finding the best in people. Her style was to embrace and work with the finer qualities in those around her—for her own benefit and for the good of her constituents, which more and more she was coming to see were all the voters of Illinois, and not just those in her district.

In 1984, Judy left the Illinois House of Representatives[78] and ran for Illinois Senate in the 22nd District.[79] She remained an Illinois state senator for two terms, but she would always miss the Illinois House—where she was able to ensure that the Ogden Avenue sewer was repaired, that needed money could go to the restoration of her favorite landmark in the Village of Lyons, Hofmann Tower,[80] that a new program for organ transplantation in Illinois could take shape, and that municipal tax reform could be a reality. Judy told Joe that she accomplished so much in the House, but she did like the four-year terms for Illinois state senators because their length provided her family a bit more stability, especially given that she was a single parent. She wouldn't have to go through as many elections as she did as a state representative.

The Illinois Senate was smaller and more formal than the House, and things there were done in a more deliberate manner. Because of its size, it was even more important to get along with people than when serving in the House of Representatives. A senator still had to maintain good relationships with fellow legislators in the House as bills go back and forth between legislative chambers before they go on to the governor for a signature.[81] Senators needed sponsors[82] for their bills in the House of Representatives, and state representatives needed sponsors for their bills in the Senate. Collegiality and compromise were even more critical for Judy as a senator. During her Senate terms,[83] Judy was able to mature as a legislator and leader who had a true understanding of what went on around the entire state of Illinois.

While in the Illinois Senate, Judy also sat on four committees[84] that came to influence her views on state finances, transportation, and law. She was on the Financial Institutions Committee, which reviewed bills dealing with banks, credit unions, and other financial institutions. The Appropriations Committee oversaw bills that proposed how tax monies would be used to pay for things within the state. The Transportation Committee oversaw roads, mass transit, and other travel-related issues. Finally, the Judiciary Committee oversaw bills proposing things within the state's legal system. Judy liked to joke with her son that the last committee made her understand lawyers and judges more than they understood themselves.

Unfortunately, the Senate was not always amicable toward women when Judy first served as a senator. She often said it was like a "good old boys' club" and women were merely tolerated. Several senior senators were known to call Judy and other women senators "babe" or "sweetie," just a couple of the disrespectful and sexist nicknames she had to put up with. She started wearing a button that instructed colleagues to call her "Senator"!

While in the Illinois Senate, Judy met two additional mentors who influenced the rest of her life in government. One was a state senator from Zion, Illinois, named Adeline Geo-Karis.[85] Adeline reminded Judy of her mother, Lillian, and Adeline pushed Judy to pursue higher office in the future. Judy loved Adeline because she was so proud of her Greek heritage,[86] very much like how Judy was proud of her Czech and Slovak heritage. The two were like "peas in a pod," and often teamed up to get various forms of legislation passed especially on matters dealing with women. They also teamed up to get a bigger bathroom for female legislators in the Senate. More importantly, Senator Geo-Karis became somewhat of a surrogate grandmother to Joe after Judy's mother died in 1987. Senator Geo-Karis, who once served in the U.S. Navy, adored Joe and took a keen interest in his efforts to become a U.S. Army officer.

Judy's other mentor was a lawyer from Oak Park, Illinois, named Phil Rock,[87] the president of the Senate. Judy liked Phil because he kept his promises. When he assured you

82

When a bill is introduced in one chamber, it is in effect sponsored by the legislator or legislators that introduce that bill in that chamber. When you read a bill, you can always read the names of the legislators who have sponsored that bill. When the bill passes one chamber, it must go to the other chamber and, again, must be introduced in that chamber by a sponsor or sponsors from that chamber. It is often good to have a bill not only sponsored by multiple sponsors but by sponsors from more than one party so that the bill has bipartisan support and is more likely to pass both chambers and go to the governor more quickly and without debate and/or objection.

83

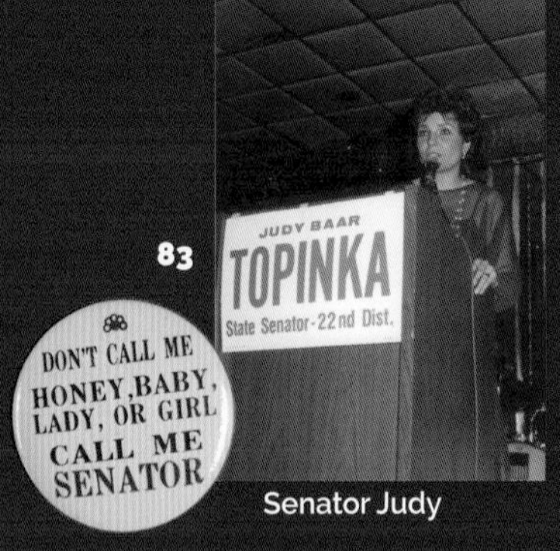

Senator Judy

84

There are committees in both the House of Representatives and the Senate. Legislators meet in these committees to review bills after they have been introduced into a particular chamber. Bills do not simply get voted upon once they are introduced. They are reviewed by the committees, whose purpose is to determine if the bills have enough merit to even be considered by the whole chamber. If run properly, they can prevent bad bills from moving forward. They can also help in improving bills.

85, 86

Judy was sworn in as treasurer by her mentor Sen. Adeline Geo-Karis

flag of Greece

87

Judy and Phil Rock

PHILIP J. ROCK

April 1996

Dear Judy,

Thank you for the kind words – it was nice to hear from you. See you I hope later this month at the Senate dinner. In the meantime quit missing newspapers — Keep up the good work Cisco. Phil

State Treasurers Office APR 9 1995 RECEIVED

88

Pages are runners who assist legislators with errands ranging from getting a cup of coffee or a sandwich to delivering correspondence. Most pages are honorary and serve for a short period of time and are sponsored by their respective legislators. Some serve for several weeks. The position affords young people, usually in high school, a bird's-eye perspective of how the legislature functions. High school students should contact their legislator's local office about their page opportunities.

Joe and his fellow pages on the Illinois House floor

SENATOR
JUDY BAAR TOPINKA

Judy's nameplate from her desk on the Senate floor

something would happen, it did. Judy liked that attitude, and it was one that she would model for the rest of her life and pass on to others.

Judy served as a legislator from 1980 to 1994. These years were some of the most educational and productive years of her life. She learned many valuable lessons.

First, she learned that constituent work is everything. The constituents are the citizens who vote for you and elect you. If they have questions or need help, they should be the top priority. Judy's constituents loved Judy because she loved them and *listened* to them. She was always willing to help them with what she called "constituent work" when they faced the bureaucracy of Illinois government on such issues as income taxes, healthcare, transportation, and even license plate renewals.

Second, Judy learned to have no fear of speaking with people and to be honest and frank about what she believed. While that was not always appreciated by some, the majority of people found it a refreshing approach. Voters may not have always liked her perspectives, but they knew where she stood on the issues, and she was willing to express those perspectives in front of all audiences, including the many youth groups she spoke to around her district. Judy saw in young people the future of the state, and she hoped her actions were good examples for the next generation.

Third, she realized the importance of being a mom, albeit a political mom. Judy took Joe on many trips to Springfield, and he eventually served as a page,[88] both in the Illinois House of Representatives and the Illinois Senate. In many ways, he grew up in the capitol—learning how ideas became laws and soaking up everything about government, especially in regard to the legislative branch. In addition, through her work, Judy showed Joe how important the state was to its citizens. The state was a source of pride to both Judy and her son. Judy taught other kids she encountered the same lessons she taught Joe, and often awarded legislative scholarships to students within her district who ultimately went on to great success later in life. One of those students was Karen Conti, who is one of the more successful attorneys practicing in Chicago today.

Fourth, Judy saw the importance of veterans' issues and the need to support reservists[89] within Illinois, especially after Joe joined the Reserve Officers Training Corps and then became a member of the Illinois National Guard. She also saw the value of military strength and the military influence on higher education within Illinois.

Finally, Judy Baar Topinka realized that her voters wanted a straight shooter when it came to the issues. She knew how to write well, and she became a good speaker; she could cut directly to the matters people wanted to hear about. People were concerned about government waste and expenditures, and Judy didn't like what she saw happening in that regard. She was vocal about it to her constituents. Her sharp writing, clear speaking, fine-tuned ability to find common ground with people, and love for her state would all come together in 1994 when Judy's final term as a legislator would end, and she began working in Illinois's executive branch.

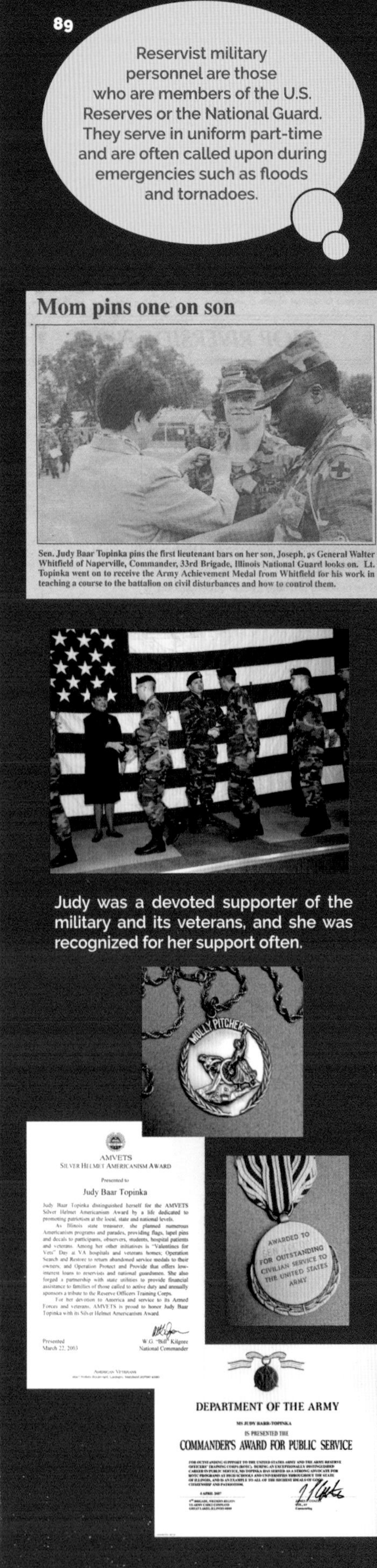

89 Reservist military personnel are those who are members of the U.S. Reserves or the National Guard. They serve in uniform part-time and are often called upon during emergencies such as floods and tornadoes.

Mom pins one on son

Sen. Judy Baar Topinka pins the first lieutenant bars on her son, Joseph, as General Walter Whitfield of Naperville, Commander, 33rd Brigade, Illinois National Guard looks on. Lt. Topinka went on to receive the Army Achievement Medal from Whitfield for his work in teaching a course to the battalion on civil disturbances and how to control them.

Judy was a devoted supporter of the military and its veterans, and she was recognized for her support often.

AMVETS
SILVER HELMET AMERICANISM AWARD

Presented to

Judy Baar Topinka

Judy Baar Topinka distinguished herself for the AMVETS Silver Helmet Americanism Award by a life dedicated to promoting patriotism at the local, state and national levels.

As Illinois state treasurer, she planned numerous Americanism programs and parades, providing flags, lapel pins and decals to participants, observers, students, hospital patients and veterans. Among her other initiatives is "Valentines for Vets" Day at VA hospitals and veterans homes; Operation Search and Restore to return abandoned service medals to their owners; and Operation Protect and Provide that offers low-interest loans to reservists and national guardsmen. She also forged a partnership with state utilities to provide financial assistance to families of those called to active duty and annually sponsors a tribute to the Reserve Officers Training Corps.

For her devotion to America and service to its Armed Forces and veterans, AMVETS is proud to honor Judy Baar Topinka with its Silver Helmet Americanism Award.

Presented
March 22, 2003

W.G. "Bill" Kilgore
National Commander

AMERICAN VETERANS

DEPARTMENT OF THE ARMY

MS JUDY BARR-TOPINKA

IS PRESENTED THE

COMMANDER'S AWARD FOR PUBLIC SERVICE

FOR OUTSTANDING SUPPORT TO THE UNITED STATES ARMY AND THE ARMY RESERVE OFFICERS' TRAINING CORPS (ROTC). DURING AN EXCEPTIONALLY DISTINGUISHED CAREER IN PUBLIC SERVICE, MS TOPINKA HAS SERVED AS A STRONG ADVOCATE FOR ROTC PROGRAMS AT HIGH SCHOOLS AND UNIVERSITIES THROUGHOUT THE STATE OF ILLINOIS, AND IS AN EXAMPLE TO ALL OF THE HIGHEST IDEALS OF GOOD CITIZENSHIP AND PATRIOTISM.

4 APRIL 2007

Resources for Further Research

Visit these sites to learn more about:

- The State of Illinois (https://www.illinois.gov/about/Pages/StateSymbols.aspx). You can find information about state symbols, state government, the state seal, and the state song.
- The Illinois State Capitol (http://www.ilstatehouse.com).
- The Illinois General Assembly through the Illinois Legislative Research Unit (http://ilga.gov/commission/lru/lru_home.html).
- The Illinois State Board of Elections (https://www.elections.il.gov). Use this site to find out who your local legislator is and in which district you are located.
- The National Conference of State Legislatures (http://www.ncsl.org). This is a great resource for comparing various state legislatures within the United States.
- Information on touring the Illinois State Capitol (https://www.cyberdriveillinois.com/departments/physical_services/captioltours.html).
- Watch both chambers of the Illinois General Assembly when they're in session (http://www.ilga.gov)!

Civics Project Ideas and Classroom Learning Activities

government institutions
current and controversial issues
service learning
democratic processes
heritage
compromise
leadership
 critical thinking

Chapter 6 Key Concepts:

- Legislating
- The Process of a Bill Becoming a Law
- Elections
- Gender Discrimination

Chapter 6 Classroom Activities (Teacher):

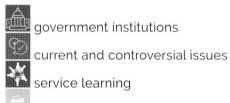

Walk students through each step (below) on how a bill becomes a law in Illinois and discuss.

1. Bill introduced in the house of origin (first house) by whom?
2. First reading of the bill.
3. Bill referred to the Rules Committee, which refers the bill to a committee of the first house.
4. Committee decides to consider the bill or not.
5. Committee or subcommittee may hold hearing(s).
6. Committee may amend the bill; committee votes to report the bill out to the first house.
7. Second reading of the bill in the first house; amendments can be proposed from the floor if they have been approved by the Rules Committee.
8. Third reading of the bill; the bill is debated and voted on.
9. The bill is sent to the second house in the form passed by the first house ("engrossed").
10. Second house repeats steps 1-8.
11. If the bill passes the second house in the same form as it is passed in the first house, it is sent to the governor. Skip to step 15.
12. If the bill passes the second house in a different version than it was passed in the first house, the second house's version is sent back to the first house to be voted on ("concurrence").
13. If the first house does not concur with the second house's version, a conference committee is formed to reconcile the differences and report back to both houses.
14. If both houses accept the conference committee report, the bill is passed and forwarded to the governor within 30 days.
15. The governor can sign or veto the bill within 60 days. If the governor does nothing, the bill becomes a law after 60 days. The governor also has the right to amend the bill ("amendatory veto") or change the dollar amount of a bill allocating funds ("item veto").
16. Both houses must vote to override a total veto by a 2/3 majority. If a total veto is not overridden, the bill dies. If an item veto is not overridden by a 2/3 majority, the bill becomes law with the change in funding proposed by the governor. If both houses override an amendatory veto, the bill becomes law in the form originally passed by both houses.
17. The law is assigned a Public Act number and printed in the Laws of Illinois.
18. Law is compiled into the Illinois Compiled Statutes (Judy Baar Topinka was involved

in the effort to reorganize Illinois laws under this current system. The ways laws are organized after passage by the legislature is a fascinating topic for research.).

19. Agencies promulgate regulations as directed in the law usually listed in the Illinois Administrative Code.

Use the photo below to discuss with students the mechanics of how legislators vote. What does each button below mean on a legislator's desk?

Chapter 6 Essay Topics (Student):

   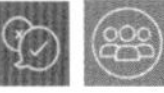

- Why are there two chambers (houses) in the Illinois General Assembly? What are the chambers called and why? How do people get elected to be in each chamber?
- Who are your local legislators? Consider writing a letter to your state representative or state senator about an issue that is important to you or consider inviting him or her to visit your class when they are in the area.
- GRADES 7–8: Select a bill that is pending in the Illinois legislature. Write about this bill and describe what steps it needs to go through in order to become a law.

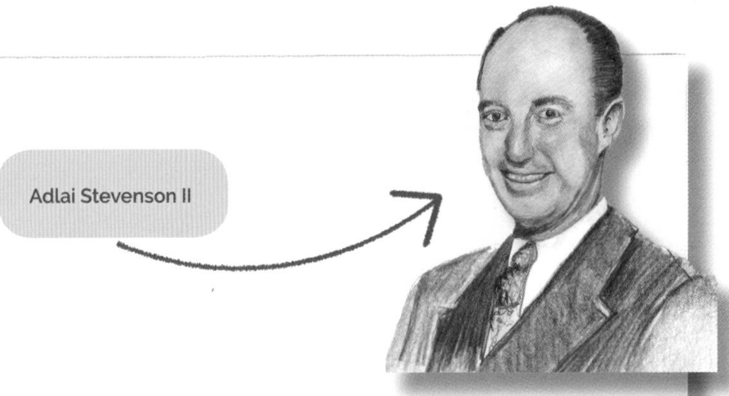

July 17, 2017

Dear Reader:

Judy Baar Topinka and I were influenced by our antecedents. My great grandfather was a US Vice-President and Congressman; my father was an Illinois Governor, Presidential candidate, and United Nations ambassador, and I was a US Senator and candidate for Illinois governor. Judy Baar Topinka's grandparents courageously came to a new country and started a small business. They raised three children, one of whom had a disability, during the Great Depression. Judy's mother, Lillian, became one of the earliest business women in a time when that was not encouraged while being a single mother with a husband, William, serving in World War II. Judy became a successful journalist, legislator, constitutional officer and parent. I sense that Judy and I looked up to our antecedents and tried to emulate their qualities on behalf of our family, community, our beloved State of Illinois and nation.

Judy was also inspired by my father. Like Judy and me, my father did not always win his political battles, but he always persevered and represented his state, his country, and dare I say the world, with wisdom and integrity. He helped make Illinois not only a power in the United States but around the world as well. I encourage you to visit the Adlai Stevenson Center on Democracy at http://stevensoncenterondemocracy.org/ and learn more about my father and the Center's activities. It carries on the fight for political reform.

Judy, like my father, loved to travel and see the world and learn about people in a way Judy would often refer to as "three dimensional learning" by seeing, hearing, tasting, touching, and smelling. She had a world view that I encourage everyone to share with Judy and my father. When Judy visited the United Nations in New York City with her son, she told him that "this place gives me hope for our world." I encourage you to visit the United Nations' website at http://www.un.org/en/index.html. It is an organization for all of us.

Never forget that you are part of many communities, and we are all citizens of the world. Embrace that world citizenship as my father and Judy Baar Topinka did. The future is global.

Sincerely,

Adlai E. Stevenson III

A Treasurer for All the People of Illinois[90]

Judy's first bill as a state senator passed on May 14, 1985.[91] While she had thought of the Illinois Senate as an old boys' club, it was in this legislative body that Judy learned more about the state of Illinois. While in the Illinois Senate, Judy began to look beyond her district and see Illinois in its entirety with all its greatness and all its challenging issues. She loved the Senate. It was smaller and more collegial than the Illinois House of Representatives. In the Senate, she met mentors who would help Judy grow and learn.

There is no doubt that Judy was loved by her constituents. In 1991, Judy received a box with a beautiful, handmade necklace from a constituent named Lieselotte Gengler. The box also contained a poem. Judy loved poetry, and this poem happened to foreshadow Judy's next political move.

A Lady Senator

By Lieselotte T. Gengler

Give us a lady that will fight
A lady with courage and scope
A lady steady as a mountain
Who believes in honor and hope.

Give us a lady to lead our future
Who is guided by heart and brain
A lady standing tall under pressure
When things go against her grain.

Give us a lady to lead us upward
Growing strong in joy and sorrow
A lady with a noble vision
Caring for a great tomorrow.

In the summer of 1992, Judy was elected for a second time to be a delegate at the Republican National Convention. The 1992 convention was in Houston, and Judy and her son packed their bags and traveled to Texas in August.[92] Judy had been elected as a delegate to attend the 1988 convention in New

90

This was Judy's motto as she ran for and became the first woman Illinois Treasurer in Illinois history. She held the office for an unprecedented three terms (twelve years).

91

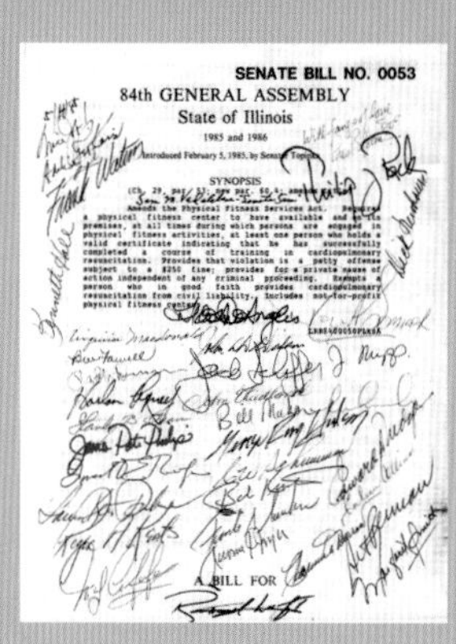

SENATE BILL NO. 0053
84th GENERAL ASSEMBLY
State of Illinois
1985 and 1986

SYNOPSIS

A BILL FOR

It was Senate Bill (SB) 53, the Physical Fitness Services Act. As was tradition in the Illinois Senate then, all the senators signed a copy of the bill and presented it to Judy.

92

At conventions, a political party brings its members together through delegates in selecting one candidate for president. It is also an opportunity to bring people together within the party at one place to talk about the issues facing the country and how the party will address those issues. Judy was delegate for George H.W. Bush at the 1988 Republican National Convention in New Orleans, Louisiana. He would lose to Bill Clinton for president in 1992.

Orleans and that was very educational for her. It taught her about the inside workings of a political party at the national level. The 1992 convention was going to take her knowledge and career to a different level.

Governor Jim Edgar wanted to talk to Judy about her future. He was setting up a "slate" for the next election. A slate is a group of political candidates who each run for a different position but normally have similar or common political interests. At the time, Governor Edgar was running for re-election for governor, the chief constitutional officer of the state as spelled out by the Illinois Constitution of 1970. There are four other constitutional office positions in Illinois: Lieutenant Governor, Attorney General, Comptroller, and Treasurer.

Governor Edgar wanted each position to be filled by someone from his party and with similar interests to his—which is what a slate is all about. He also wanted the speaker of the House of Representatives and the president of the Senate to be of the same party. While these were not constitutional office positions, Governor Edgar unofficially included his choices for those positions on his slate. To be elected, those choices had to be made by a majority of legislators from each house. Edgar was sending a clear message that he intended Republican majorities in both legislative houses so that a Republican speaker and president would be elected.

Judy knew something was up, especially after her son and the governor's son were introduced to each other at the convention. The two sons got along and Judy guessed that Governor Edgar was considering how his family and hers could get along if he and Judy ran as a team.[93] Judy was thinking that Edgar would ask her to be his running mate, to be lieutenant governor. In Illinois, the governor and lieutenant governor run as a team like the president and vice-president of the United States run as a team. It would have been a great honor to be the first woman lieutenant governor of Illinois, but Governor Edgar chose another man who also had served as a legislator just as Judy had done. Instead, the idea was developed that Judy should run for Illinois State Treasurer. As someone who

93

The governor and lieutenant governor had always run as a team in Illinois, though both people do not have to be nominated as a team under the Illinois Constitution of 1970. This little known aspect of the Illinois Constitution made a great impact in March 1986 when two followers of a far-right conservative party led by Lyndon H. LaRouche (pictured above) ran as Democrats in primary elections for the lieutenant governor and secretary of state positions. Senator Adlai E. Stevenson, III, grandson of the former vice-president of the United States and son of the former governor and ambassador to the United Nations, Adlai Stevenson II, found himself with a running mate not of his choice nor in support of his interests. Senator Stevenson would go on to lose the general election against Governor James R. Thompson. He chose not to run with the candidate affiliated with Lyndon LaRouche's organization and instead ran in a party he named the Solidarity Party. Jim Edgar would win the election for secretary of state that year, setting him up for a future as governor of Illinois years later.

Jim Edgar

grew up in a frugal, Czech family that knew the importance of saving money, the position seemed to be a natural one for her.

Running for a statewide office was a big move, and Judy needed buy-in from her then remaining family members: her father and her son. Her father, Bill, had not been well, had just been through an operation, and was recovering at a rehabilitation facility on Ogden Avenue in Cicero. Her son was studying for the Illinois bar exam and also preparing to go on active duty in the U.S. Army. They all met in the rehabilitation facility and talked over the pros and cons of stepping into this bigger arena. They all agreed it was the right choice. Once again, Ogden Avenue would serve a role in Judy's life during a major decision![94]

Campaigning for the office of Illinois state treasurer was one of the biggest challenges of Judy's career. There's no way around it—Illinois is a big state to cover. Her son and others campaigned with her around the state, usually driving her in a van.[95] They all ate a lot of fast food and, in some parts of the state, they ate a lot of ham and beans—both of which could cause some extreme stomach problems in this fast-paced lifestyle. Campaign funds were tight, so Joe would often collect unused campaign brochures and posters from one event and re-use them at another.

After the successful March 15, 1994, primary, the slate took on its now recognized appearance. It was the Republican team that was going to win in the general election in November 1994. The team met on March 16, 1994, in Chicago and stood for a now famous photo that Judy would keep close for many years thereafter. She, along with many other people around the state, felt that the Republican Party in Illinois was on the right track.[96] Judy's son left shortly afterwards for service in the U.S. Army.[97] Judy won the election in November, but it was a bittersweet moment. Judy's father couldn't attend the celebration that election night because of his immobility, and her son could not get leave from the Army to join her. In addition, her cousin, Miloslav Matouškova (known to everyone as Slava) in Prague had promised Judy he would

94

The road had a great history as being one of the earliest roads going from Chicago to the suburbs of Chicago. Ogden Avenue began in 1848 as a road composed of planks that made traffic across the swampy ground between Chicago and Riverside possible. It was first named Plank Road and later was named after the first mayor of Chicago, William B. Ogden.

95

Judy had a license plate spelling "TOPINKA" for the van. See it on page 56.

96

The famous photo

97

Joe first went to the Quartermaster School at Fort Lew, Virginia, in Spring 1994 and then became a military attorney attending the Judge Advocate General's School in Charlottesville, Virginia, in fall 1994. His first active duty assignment began in the winter of 1994 at Fort Wainwright, Alaska, near Fairbanks.

attend election night. He even purchased a special suit for the occasion but passed away just months before in August.

Every public official must be sworn into office, as it is required by law.[98] Judy had been sworn in as a legislator four times. But being sworn in as the first woman to be state treasurer in Illinois history was different. This was a lot bigger, and the ceremony was at a bigger place because it was more historic, as she was being sworn in along with the governor. Constitutional office holders are usually sworn in at the Prairie State Convention Center in Springfield, Illinois.[99] It was huge and a little overwhelming for Judy. She was nervous and continued to work on her speech until she walked onto the stage. Her father, Bill, now wheelchair bound, was transported from Riverside. Her son, who was then in Alaska, traveled the farthest of anyone that day to attend the ceremony. Since Judy's mom had passed away in 1987, one of Judy's mentors from the Senate, Adeline Geo-Karis, filled in for her mother and actually read Judy the oath of office.[100] She was truly surrounded by family, albeit a very little family.

As the state treasurer is the lowest ranking position of all the constitutional office positions, Judy was last to get sworn in and the last to speak. As one reporter noted, there was much exuberance at the event but no one expected Judy's quip about enduring ham-and-bean dinners while campaigning in a small van. The audience reacted with incredible laughter to that one! It was this speech that demonstrated Judy's self-deprecating humor and her humbleness to a state-wide audience. Following Judy's speech, Jennifer Halperin of *Illinois Issues* wrote that Judy was "The GOP's sassiest pol" in the March 10, 1995, issue.[101] Who was this "sassy" lady, they asked? Judy made the following statement to Ms. Halperin: "I think a lot of Republicans look at me as an eccentric, an aberration—the king's fool....What people forget is that the king's fool used to have a major role in making policy." People may have thought Illinois State Treasurer Judy Baar Topinka was the king's fool because of her efforts to repair a sewer or to save former President Grant's tomb in New York City, but

98 Section 3 of Article 13 of the Illinois Constitution of 1970 states that each prospective holder of a state office or other state position created by the constitution, before taking office, shall take and subscribe to the following oath or affirmation: "I do solemnly swear (affirm) that I will support the Constitution of the United States, and the Constitution of the State of Illinois, and that I will faithfully discharge the duties of the office of .... to the best of my ability."

99

Prairie State Convention Center

100 State Senator Adeline Geo-Karis, a Republican from Zion, Illinois, was honored to substitute for Judy's mother on that Monday, January 9, 1995. She was a personal friend of Judy's mother, Lillian, and a vocally proud ethnic Greek-American who served with Judy during her two terms as state senator. Judy was always a fan of classical Greek literature and ancient Greek history. Judy stated at the time: "Like the ancients, I wanted to go to Delphi in Greece before my first election to the post of state representative...and...bring a shiny new Susan B. Anthony dollar and slip it through the crack at the site of the Oracle [of Delphi]. The dollar in the crack would be "proof an American woman could successfully run for office in a democracy in the Greek tradition."

101

Illinois Issues, March 1995. The word pol is a short form of the word politician.

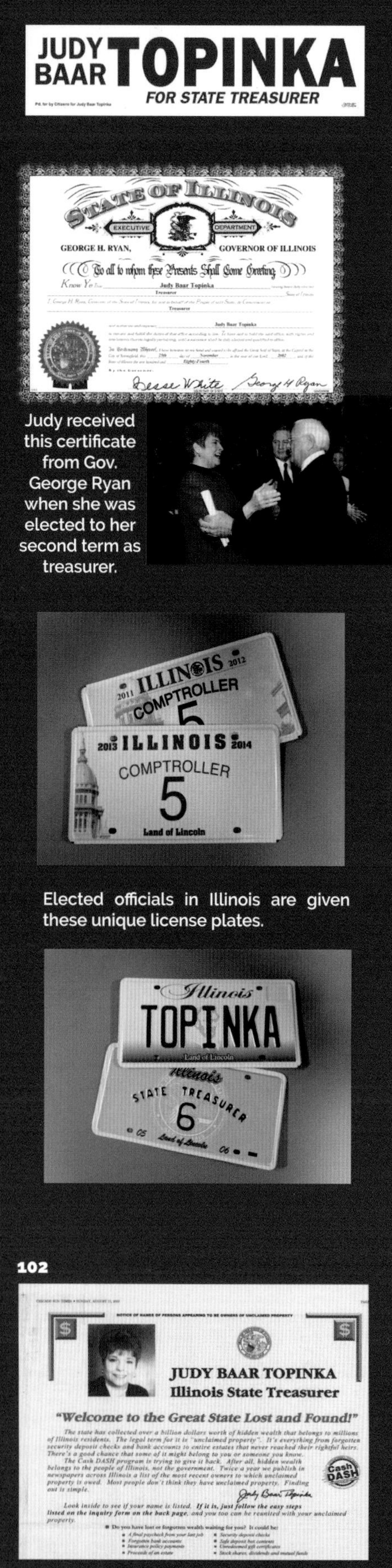

Judy received this certificate from Gov. George Ryan when she was elected to her second term as treasurer.

Elected officials in Illinois are given these unique license plates.

102

those who initially misjudged her were to find themselves wrong and very short-sighted.

Judy set out to make the Illinois State Treasurer's office a model for state treasurers around the country. She knew that most people only focused on the more visible positions in government like governor, senator, and president, but she also knew that the majority of work is done at the lower levels. She learned that lesson by watching municipal government leaders as a reporter, and as a legislator focusing on the day-to-day issues of her constituents. She took that perspective and applied it to the years she served as treasurer, creating some incredible programs for people, many of which continue today.

During the first eight years as state treasurer, Judy was able to move the outdated unclaimed assets system from the governor's office with the help of then-Governor George H. Ryan. Illinois, like other states, has a system in place in which unclaimed property goes to the state and is maintained by the state sometimes for a period of time that seems like forever or until the rightful owner or heirs come forward to claim the property. Unclaimed property consists of things like bank accounts, uncashed checks, old military medals, and jewelry that is being held at companies, banks, courts, and life insurance companies and have gone unclaimed for a specific period of time. Judy's office upgraded the program electronically so that millions of Illinois citizens had an easier way to claim the items, in most cases money, that were due to them.[102] Judy called the program Cash Dash, and people in Illinois loved it because they could find lost items that in some cases people did not even know were lost. Judy's son even found uncashed dividend checks from stock that he inherited from his grandfather. Cash Dash was an extraordinary success. The program returned more property to the public in six years than the combined total for the twenty-seven years the program was run by the governor's office.

Judy understood the challenges that faced families paying for college. Judy was so proud of Joe for receiving a scholarship for college through the U.S. Army's Reserve Officer Training Corps. She was relieved that the award would cover his tuition, but it didn't pay for all of Joe's bills at the University of Illinois. Judy and her son had been saving for his college education for years, just like other families around Illinois did. She started wondering, *how could saving for college be easier and generate more money for families?* Judy began a program called the Bright Start College Savings Program. It was and still is a college savings program run by the Illinois state treasurer's office. The program allows families to save money toward a student's education and pay no taxes on any earnings made by the funds invested in the account. When it is time to go to college, withdrawals from the account are tax-free as long as they go to eligible educational expenses. The money can be used at in-state, out-of-state, vocational, community, and private institutions. It was an incredibly valuable program for young people and, while Judy was treasurer, 130,000 families saved more than $1.7 million to pay for college.[103] People around Illinois began to recognize Judy from all the Bright Start television commercials that were made and aired. Some criticized that they were merely political self-promotion. But Judy just wanted to get the word out on saving money for college and enjoyed working with the kids that helped her do the TV spots. She loved these commercials!

Judy talked both publicly and privately about her family's heritage as frugal, how Czech-Americans saved money however they could, but she never really learned about managing her own personal finances when she was young—and when it would have been important to have those skills. She believed that young people, especially in fifth and sixth grades, needed to learn about managing their money so that they could make wise financial choices as they got older. She promoted the Illinois state treasurer's Bank at School program, which contained lesson plans and exercises designed to introduce students to the world of money and banking. The program was a success and was also used to teach older students and even adults. The program helped more than 270,000 Illinois schoolchildren understand personal finance better.[104]

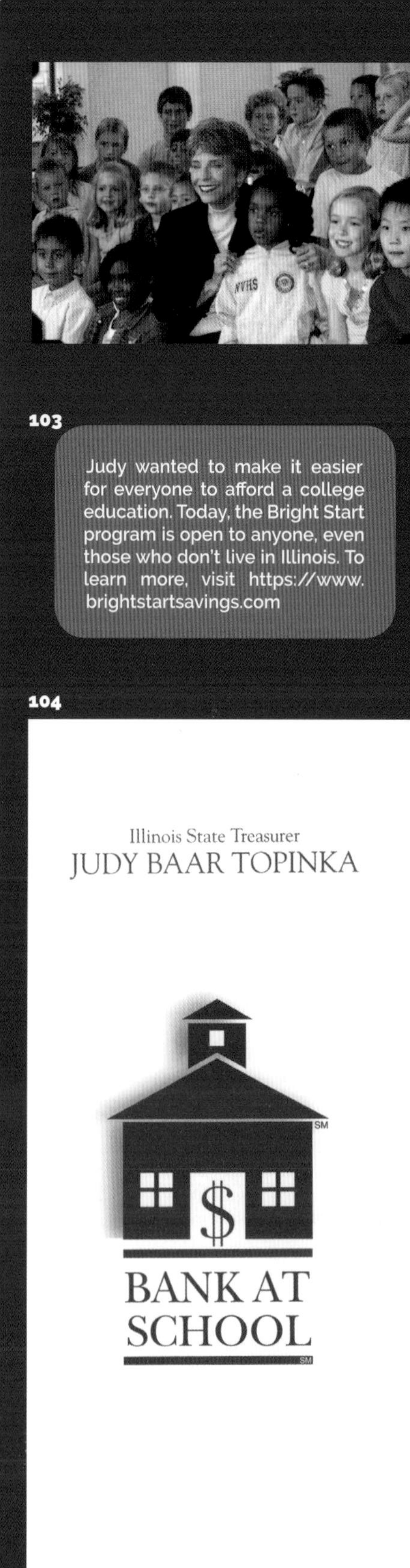

103

Judy wanted to make it easier for everyone to afford a college education. Today, the Bright Start program is open to anyone, even those who don't live in Illinois. To learn more, visit https://www.brightstartsavings.com

104

Her continued love for animals inspired Judy to create the Treasurer's Treasured Pets Program to help Illinoisans adopt pets and to save the state money by not having to euthanize those animals.[105] The program was part of her lifelong effort to link people to no-kill animal shelters. The idea resulted from a visit to the Sangamon County pound in 2001 to help a co-worker pick a new dog. Judy not only ended up choosing a dog named Andy to adopt, but she decided to launch a program to encourage these adoptions. It made her feel good, it made others feel good, it saved the lives of many animals, and it in fact saved the state money.

Finally, Judy succeeded in taking taxpayer money and using it to make more money for the state through various types of investments. One such way was through the Illinois Public Treasurer's Investment Pool, call IPTIP, which especially helps local governments pool their funds for investment and then returns greater earnings on those investments. The fund was consistently given a AAA rating by Standard and Poor's since it was such a strong and solid investment pool for those governments.[106]

Judy did so many other things while she was treasurer, and many of those things focused on promoting a sense of Illinois history for its citizens. For example, she was involved in the design of the Illinois quarter for the U.S. Mint's 50 State Quarters Program to ensure it reflected the greatness of Illinois's past.[107] She oversaw the design and issuance of a series of medallions authorized by the legislature in 2001 honoring Abraham Lincoln, Ulysses S. Grant, Ronald Reagan, Governor Adlai Stevenson, and Mayor Harold Washington. Each of these leaders inspired Judy and, in her words, the coins "[a]dvance[d] the cause of Illinois history." She continued her work begun as a legislator in the cause of moving President Grant's tomb to Galena, Illinois, where he once lived. Grant's tomb, which is now formally known as General Grant National Memorial, has been in New York City since it was completed in 1897. In the 1990s, Judy became very upset by the condition of the memorial as unsuitable for one of Illinois's greatest citizens.

105 Judy was a great supporter of many animal groups. She especially loved PAWS-Chicago. PAWS stands for Progressive Animal Welfare Society (PAWS) and it is a model used around the country for no-kill animal shelters. Judy frequently donated money and time in support of its no-kill advocacy and care of animals.

106 Standard and Poor's is an American financial company that publishes financial research and analysis and is considered one of the big three credit-rating agencies along with Moody's Investment Service and Fitch Ratings. A triple A (AAA) rating is the highest credit rating that Standard and Poor's can assign. In other words, these company's ratings indicate to investors what the level of return from their investment will be. A high return will yield a high rating. A low return, if any, will result in a low or absent rating.

107

The Illinois quarter depicts a young Abraham Lincoln within the outline of the state. A farm scene and the Chicago skyline appear on the left and to the right of the state's outline. Twenty-one stars border the coin, signifying Illinois as the 21st state to be admitted into the Union on December 3, 1818.

The memorial was covered with graffiti and surrounded by litter. The National Park Service refurbished the site to its current pristine condition as a result of Judy's call for action.[108] And Judy also continued her efforts begun as a legislator to support the Wolf Road Prairie program in Westchester, Illinois, because its closeness to the very congested city of Chicago and its location in Cook County made it an important part of Illinois's natural history.[109]

Judy's last term as treasurer for the state of Illinois was a challenging one. Of all the politicians that had been in the 1994 Republican Team picture taken in Chicago, Judy was the only one left; she was the only Republican constitutional office holder in Illinois. As the senior-most elected Republican official in the state, she became by default the Republican leader of Illinois. She decided, therefore, to take on the role of the Illinois Republican Party chairman, thereby becoming the first female Republican chairman in the state's history. This political role would cause her great stress and grief, especially when she found herself trying to find a candidate to run against a popular state senator by the name of Barack Obama. She could not find anyone interested in the undertaking. At one point, those around her suggested she run against Obama. She had more experience than he did, and she was liked by people all over the state. However, Judy had no desire to go to Washington, D.C. Besides, she was more concerned about another person that was causing the state problems.

A new governor had been elected in Illinois, and his name was Rod Blagojevich. He was from Chicago and related by marriage to Chicago alderman Richard F. "Dick" Mel.[110] Judy believed the new governor was dishonest. Just prior to her third inaugural ceremony, Judy, her new daughter-in-law, Christina, and her son were sitting in the First United Methodist Church in Springfield during the traditional prayer service held prior to the inauguration in the Prairie State Convention Center. Judy leaned over to Joe, who was on leave from his assignment at the U.S. Army's Judge Advocate General's School, and said, "That man (nodding to Rod Blagojevich) is bad and cannot

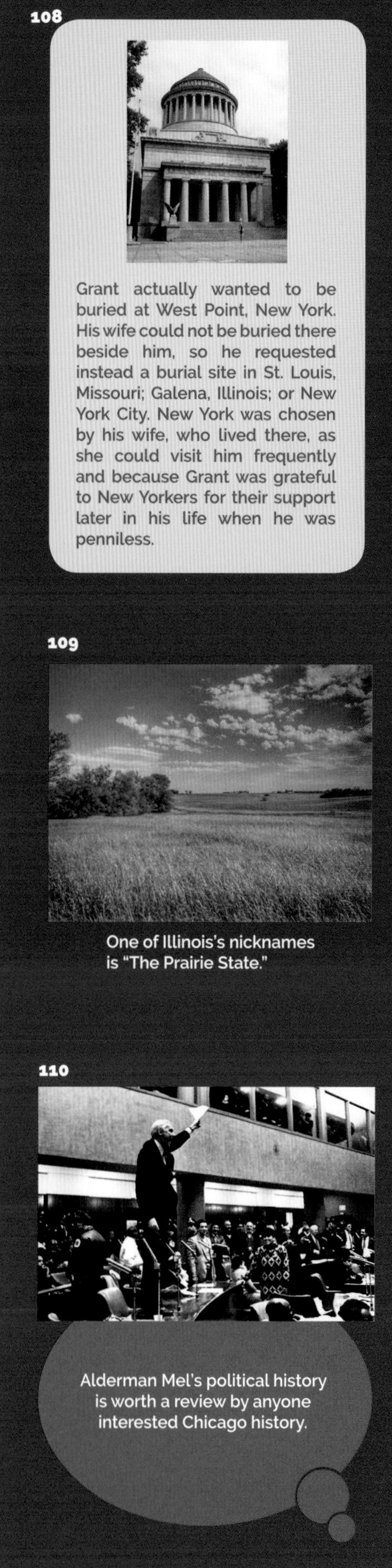

108 Grant actually wanted to be buried at West Point, New York. His wife could not be buried there beside him, so he requested instead a burial site in St. Louis, Missouri; Galena, Illinois; or New York City. New York was chosen by his wife, who lived there, as she could visit him frequently and because Grant was grateful to New Yorkers for their support later in his life when he was penniless.

109 One of Illinois's nicknames is "The Prairie State."

110 Alderman Mel's political history is worth a review by anyone interested Chicago history.

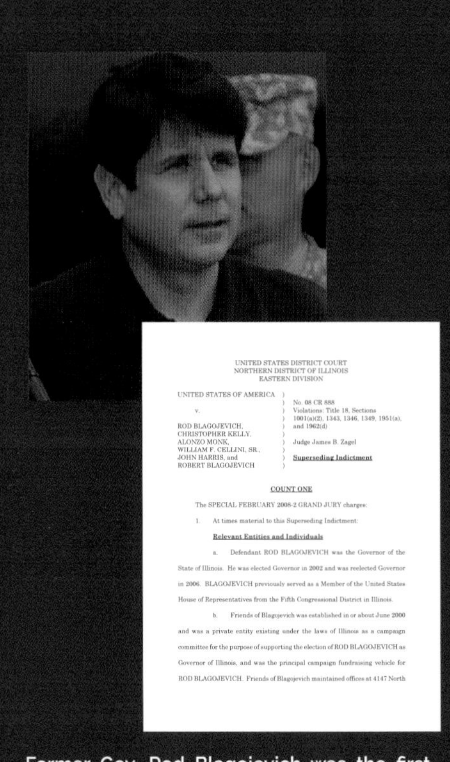

UNITED STATES DISTRICT COURT
NORTHERN DISTRICT OF ILLINOIS
EASTERN DIVISION

UNITED STATES OF AMERICA) No. 08 CR 888
v.) Violations: Title 18, Sections 1001(a)(2), 1343, 1346, 1349, 1951(a), and 1962(d)
ROD BLAGOJEVICH, CHRISTOPHER KELLY, ALONZO MONK, WILLIAM F. CELLINI, SR., JOHN HARRIS, and ROBERT BLAGOJEVICH) Judge James B. Zagel

Superseding Indictment

COUNT ONE

The SPECIAL FEBRUARY 2008-2 GRAND JURY charges:

1. At times material to this Superseding Indictment:

Relevant Entities and Individuals

a. Defendant ROD BLAGOJEVICH was the Governor of the State of Illinois. He was elected Governor in 2002 and was reelected Governor in 2006. BLAGOJEVICH previously served as a Member of the United States House of Representatives from the Fifth Congressional District in Illinois.

b. Friends of Blagojevich was established in or about June 2000 and was a private entity existing under the laws of Illinois as a campaign committee for the purpose of supporting the election of ROD BLAGOJEVICH as Governor of Illinois, and was the principal campaign fundraising vehicle for ROD BLAGOJEVICH. Friends of Blagojevich maintained offices at 4147 North

Former Gov. Rod Blagojevich was the first governor in Illinois history to be removed from office. Above is the first page of the list of crimes he was charged with.

Blagojevich's trial took place at the Everett McKinley Dirksen United States Courthouse in Chicago.

Blagojevich's is currently serving his sentence at the Federal Correctional Institution in Englewood, Colorado, and isn't scheduled to be released until 2024.

be trusted." Joe said with a smile, "Well, Mom, he may be dishonest but at least he dresses well."

Years later, after Rod Blagojevich became the first Illinois governor to be removed from office, and after he was convicted and sent to federal prison, people would learn that Joe was correct, he was well dressed. His suits cost thousands of dollars and questions arose about where he received the money to buy them. Years later, people would also realize that what Judy said to her son was also correct—but that realization would come too late for Judy and for Illinois.

In the meantime, Judy found herself facing a major question: *What will I do next?* She was now the only Republican leader in Illinois left standing; she was the Republican state chairman responsible for getting the vote out for various candidates at the state and local levels, many of whom she did not like; and she was trying to work with a governor whose lack of integrity, commitment, and focus on state issues was toxic.

Lieselotte Gengler's poem was correct. Illinois needed a lady to fight for its future and lead it well. Judy Baar Topinka was that woman and many believed Judy was the person to stop this governor. Judy had to decide what her next step would be. Her decision would be the biggest gamble she ever took, and its outcome will be forever second-guessed by Illinois citizens.

Resources for Further Research

Visit these sites to learn more about State of Illinois programs:

- Unclaimed assets in Illinois: https://icash.illinoistreasurer.gov.
- College savings in Illinois: https://www.brightstartsavings.com/OFI529.
- PAWS Chicago: http://www.pawschicago.org.
- Illinois Issues: http://illinoisissues.uis.edu/about.

Visit these sites to learn more about Illinois history:

- Illinois Commemorative Medallion Program: https://store.nwtmint.com/Historical/Illinois.
- Illinois State Archives: http://www.cyberdriveillinois.com/departments/archives/home.html.
- Illinois State Historical Society: http://www.historyillinois.org.
- Information about visiting President Grant's tomb can be found through the National Park Service at: https://www.nps.gov/gegr/index.htm. Information about Grant's Galena, Illinois, home is at: http://www.granthome.com.
- Information on Governor and Ambassador Adlai Stevenson, II is located at: http://www.adlaitoday.org/ideas/adlai_exhibits.html. He is buried in Evergreen Memorial Cemetery in Bloomington, Illinois.

Get to know about the natural beauty and natural history of Illinois, and especially the Wolf Road Prairie, at the following locations:

- Save the Prairie Society: http://savetheprairiesociety.org.
- Salt Creek Greenway Association: http://saltcreekgreenwayassociation.org/files/wolfroadprairie.html.
- Forest Preserves of Cook County: http://fpdcc.com/location/wolf-road-prairie.
- Illinois Department of Natural Resources: http://www.dnr.illinois.gov/INPC/Pages/Area2CookWolfRoadPrairie.aspx.

Get to understand banking and financing at these sites that Judy liked:

- U.S. Federal Reserve: https://www.federalreserveeducation.org.
- Museum of American Finance: http://www.moaf.org/education/index.
- Bureau of Engraving and Printing: http://www.moneyfactory.com.
- International Monetary Fund: http://www.imf.org/external/index.htm.
- U.S. Department of the Treasury: https://www.treasury.gov/Pages/default.aspx.
- World Bank: http://www.worldbank.org.
- Chicago Mercantile Exchange: http://www.cmegroup.com.
- Securities Industry and Financial Markets Association: http://www.sifma.org.

Civics Project Ideas and Classroom Learning Activities

government institutions
current and controversial issues
service learning
democratic processes
heritage
compromise
leadership
critical thinking

Chapter 7 Key Concepts:

- Financial Literacy
- Money Management
- Investment
- Assets
- Promises and Oaths
- Politics

Chapter 7 Classroom Activities (Teacher):

- Review with students the job of a treasurer. How does a treasurer use and make decisions about money the way an individual, family, or business does?
- Ask students about the money they may have. Where does it come from? Do they save any? Why or why not?
- Have students visit the Illinois treasurer online and search the Cash Dash website to see if they or their family members have any unclaimed assets. Define "unclaimed asset" and discuss some examples.

Chapter 7 Essay Topics (Student):

- Look up the Illinois Constitution of 1970 and read about the role of the Illinois state treasurer. Write about why a state has a state treasurer and his or her role in good governance.
- GRADES 7–8: Why do government leaders take an oath of office? Under what circumstances do you make promises? Write about promises and oaths of office. Why are they important?

Governor Judy?

Figuring out what she was going to do next in her political career was not going to be easy for Judy. The decision came during a very turbulent time in Illinois during Judy's third term as Illinois state treasurer. Not only was her holding this position for a third term unprecedented in Illinois, but by default, Judy was the new leader of the Illinois Republican Party and she was stepping into another first—becoming the first female chairman of the Illinois Republican Party.

Judy and the party were soon facing a complicated U.S. Senate campaign when Republican candidate Jack Ryan had to drop out of the race due to a family scandal. The Illinois Republican Central Committee[111] voted to then support Alan Keyes, an outspoken conservative politician from Maryland,[112] to run against Barack Obama[113], a relatively new Illinois state senator who had made a big impression during a speech he gave at the 2004 Democratic National Convention. Most people don't realize that the central committee is made up of representatives from each congressional district of Illinois. Each has his or her own separate vote on matters. The majority of the membership voted for Keyes. Judy was against the choice of Keyes—and she avoided all contact with him during the election—but as chairman she was blamed for his selection.

The U.S. Senate race in Illinois was unpleasant, and it foreshadowed how disagreeable the Republican primary and general election for governor would be in two years. Judy's son had deployed to Afghanistan around this time for a short period until he became very ill. He wouldn't see his mother for about a year after his return. When he did, it was in a hotel suite in New York City at the 2004 Republican Convention. Both Joe and Christina were surprised by how much weight his mother had lost. The Ryan/Keyes/Obama election had taken its toll on Judy's health and they were now very concerned about her. Ironically, Judy was concerned about Joe's health, as it would never be the same after his deployment.

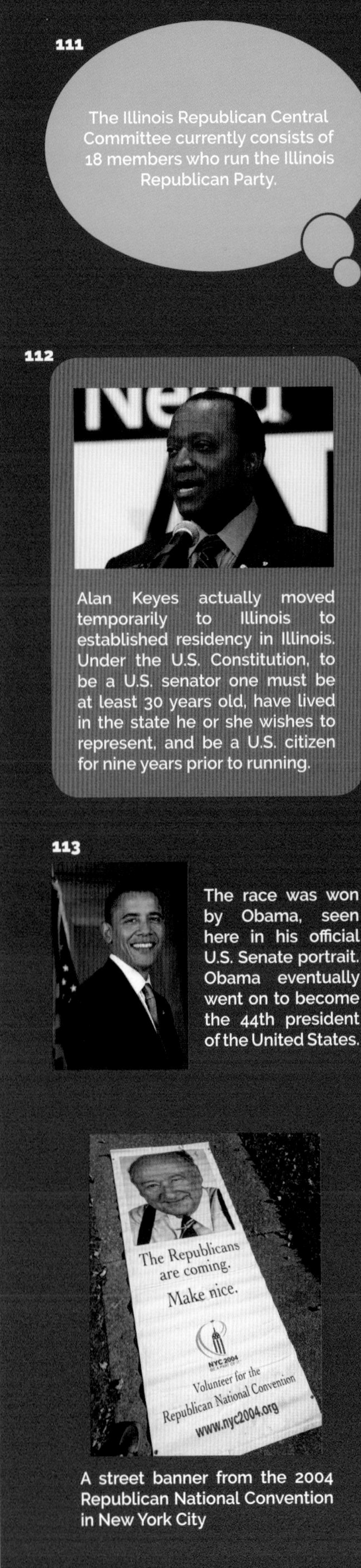

111 The Illinois Republican Central Committee currently consists of 18 members who run the Illinois Republican Party.

112 Alan Keyes actually moved temporarily to Illinois to established residency in Illinois. Under the U.S. Constitution, to be a U.S. senator one must be at least 30 years old, have lived in the state he or she wishes to represent, and be a U.S. citizen for nine years prior to running.

113 The race was won by Obama, seen here in his official U.S. Senate portrait. Obama eventually went on to become the 44th president of the United States.

A street banner from the 2004 Republican National Convention in New York City

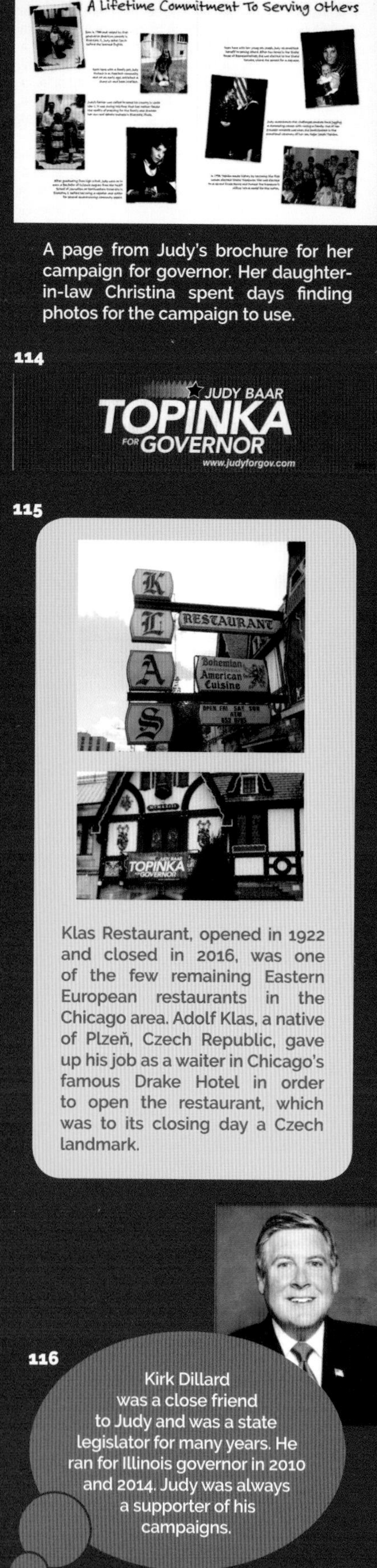

A page from Judy's brochure for her campaign for governor. Her daughter-in-law Christina spent days finding photos for the campaign to use.

114

115

Klas Restaurant, opened in 1922 and closed in 2016, was one of the few remaining Eastern European restaurants in the Chicago area. Adolf Klas, a native of Plzeň, Czech Republic, gave up his job as a waiter in Chicago's famous Drake Hotel in order to open the restaurant, which was to its closing day a Czech landmark.

116

Kirk Dillard was a close friend to Judy and was a state legislator for many years. He ran for Illinois governor in 2010 and 2014. Judy was always a supporter of his campaigns.

For the next two years, Joe was reassigned to Washington state. He talked with his mom by telephone countless times about her running for governor. Judy was deferential to former governor Jim Edgar. Rumors floated around Illinois that he would run against Governor Blagojevich. Joe secretly hoped that Jim Edgar would in fact run against Blagojevich, whom he had come to distrust based on all the stories in the Illinois newspapers about his conduct in office. Jim Edgar decided not to run and encouraged Judy to run instead. Over a phone call to Joe and Christina in late summer 2005, Judy made the decision to run. She sent Joe a bumper sticker in the mail that read "Judy Baar Topinka for Governor." As soon as Joe saw it, he called her. Judy commented that it was kind of "freaky" that her name was on the bumper sticker with the word "Governor."[114] Joe agreed that it was strange, but he told his mom that they loved her and would support her as always.

Illinois Treasurer Judy Baar Topinka announced her candidacy for governor days later on November 7, 2005, at the Klas Czech Restaurant[115] in Cicero, Illinois, demonstrating her pride in her Czech and Slovak heritage just as she had done back in 1979. Unfortunately, the Czech restaurant where she first announced her candidacy for Illinois State Representative had burned down years earlier. Kirk Dillard[116] was the master of ceremonies and Joe was the first speaker on behalf of his mom. He spoke about how great Judy was but for the fact she could barely cook, even Hamburger Helper being a challenge for her. Joe shared his mother's sense of humor and the audience laughed.

Judy, Joe, Christina, and several other people, along with Judy's dog Molly, flew around the state making the same speeches over a two-day period. The U.S. military has specific ethics rules about military personnel being involved in political campaigns, so Joe had to ensure that his family ties with his mother did not cross the political lines described in military regulations. Therefore, Joe had special permission from the U.S. Army to travel with his mother, not as a member of the military, but only in a personal capacity, as Judy's son. Together they visited Rockford, Peoria, Springfield, Carbondale, and several other communities in Illinois. It was exhausting, but the announcement was made. Judy now faced four other candidates in the Republican primary. Just as when she first ran for office as a state legislator, all of her opponents were male.[117]

Like the U.S. Senate election two years earlier, the Republican primary was not cordial and, in many respects, it was outright disrespectful. Both Rod Gidwitz and Jim Oberweis were extremely rude to Judy in public. When Gidwitz ran several offensive primary television ads against Judy, he was officially rebuked by the Illinois Republican Party as his advertisements violated the party's code of conduct.[118] Oberweis's TV ads against Judy were criticized for frequently imposing false headlines on the images of Illinois newspapers, and his advertisements were also reviewed by the Illinois Republican Party. Several television stations withdrew these political commercials. Judy felt both candidates' treatment of her was sexist at best. Sexism is when someone treats another differently because of their gender. Judy told her son that she could never forget Oberweis, as his behavior during the primary was the worst she had ever seen displayed by a candidate for public office in Illinois.

Judy won the primary[119] with 37 percent of the vote. She was the first woman Republican in Illinois history to be nominated for the position of governor. Joe could not get military leave to attend the election night celebration, but daughter-in-law Christina filled in and brought a video recorded by Joe congratulating his mother. Joe had made two videos: one to show if she won and one to show if she lost. He was happy that she won, but he feared the general election that was to come. Joe had been an ethics counselor in the U.S. Army for over a decade, and he knew how nasty an election could be against a sitting governor whose integrity was in question.

As expected, the general election was also very unpleasant. Judy reflected years later that there was really only one truly public debate between herself and Rod Blagojevich. It was on Dick Kay's City Desk program in April 2006, WMAQ-TV,

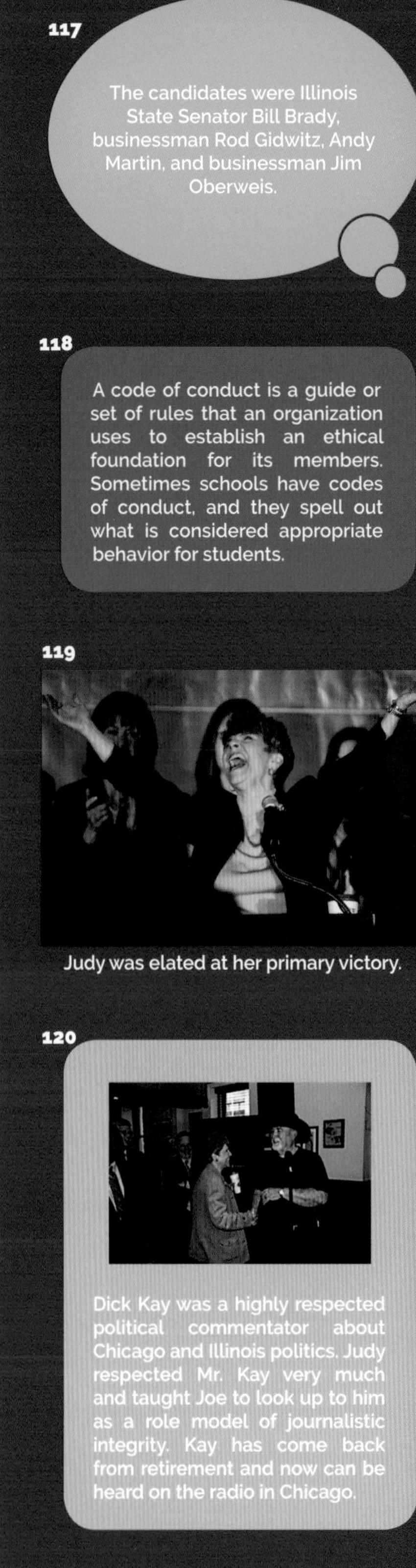

117
The candidates were Illinois State Senator Bill Brady, businessman Rod Gidwitz, Andy Martin, and businessman Jim Oberweis.
118
A code of conduct is a guide or set of rules that an organization uses to establish an ethical foundation for its members. Sometimes schools have codes of conduct, and they spell out what is considered appropriate behavior for students.
119
120
Dick Kay was a highly respected political commentator about Chicago and Illinois politics. Judy respected Mr. Kay very much and taught Joe to look up to him as a role model of journalistic integrity. Kay has come back from retirement and now can be heard on the radio in Chicago.

Judy was elated at her primary victory.

Channel 5, in Chicago.[120] It was Kay's last show before he retired in June. Judy outperformed Blagojevich, and there was never a televised public debate again.[121]

Judy campaigned all over the state and ran a positive election, but she simply didn't have enough funding. Many right wing conservatives[122] within the Republican Party did not support her due to her views on gay rights and women's rights. Many people still blamed her over the failed U.S. Senate election that brought Barack Obama into office. Then, a Green Party candidate[123] entered the general election. He was getting support, but no one knew from where. Judy always wondered if many of the conservative members of her party were supporting this Green Party candidate behind the scenes because they did not like her. Sometimes people support candidates that counteract the candidates they do not want to win an election. These candidates are often called "spoilers." It was a belief that saddened Judy. It meant members of her own party were in effect helping Blagojevich win. Blagojevich didn't campaign much, but he didn't have to. He had millions of dollars in campaign funding, and he spent that money on commercials in the biggest market in Illinois: Chicago. He outspent her three to one in terms of millions of dollars. As Judy used to say, if you win Chicago, you win Illinois. The Blagojevich commercials were mean and painted Judy as incompetent, often asking to make their point: "What was she thinking?" The ads actually helped make Judy better known than Blagojevich, but in a very negative way, and they hurt her emotionally. What TV commercials Judy was able to fund were always positive.

During the election, Judy continued to state that Blagojevich was "Suspect X" and was being investigated by the U.S. Attorney's Office in Chicago. She knew he was dirty and that there were always questions about where he was getting money to fund his campaign. Judy secretly hoped that he would be federally indicted.[124] It never happened during the campaign. To the very end, she argued that he was a "pay-to-play"[125] governor and expected people to pay him for any

121

JACK HIGGINS' OPINION

Cartoon of Judy after the debate

122

Political parties often have different parts or "wings" that can be more or less liberal, moderate, or conservative. Often, it is difficult to determine what these labels mean. Judy taught Joe that understanding the wings was like looking at a scale. If you are in the middle, you are moderate and balanced. If you are on the left of the scale or the right of the scale, the scale leans in that direction. Judy considered herself a conservative in the Republican Party when it came to financial issues but a moderate when it came to social issues.

123

There are many political parties in the United States. We often hear about the Republican and Democratic parties, but there are others like the Green Party, which supports peace and non-violence, ecological wisdom, grassroots democracy, and social justice.

124

An indictment is a formal accusation that a person committed a crime. In most states and at the federal level, it is usually done for felonies, the most serious of crimes. Usually, an indictment is handed down by a grand jury, which is a group of people brought together to investigate potential criminal conduct and to determine if charges should be brought against someone. It is a separate type of jury from those seen in courts and can be done at the state and federal levels.

political favors he provided through his position as governor.

Judy had very little money for her campaign. Massachusetts Governor Mitt Romney had promised Judy hundreds of thousands of dollars in his position as Chairman of the National Governor's Association, but he never gave her those funds. She never forgave him for that and would not support him years later when he ran for president. President George W. Bush held a fundraiser for Judy, and First Lady Laura Bush also hosted a fundraiser for her. Both events together raised more than $1 million for her campaign,[126] but it wasn't enough to go up against the almost $20 million Rod Blagojevich had. Judy figured if she worked hard and campaigned like she always did, then people would vote for her. She learned that money and commercials are more important. As much as she tried to get donations from supporters, there simply was not enough coming in to compete with Blagojevich's campaign war chest.[127]

Judy's son Joe called her every day from Washington during her campaign for governor, sometimes three times a day. He nagged her constantly to have an Illinois state trooper escort her, because some people had said some crazy things to her that could be interpreted as threats. Judy refused the Illinois State Police protective detail she had been offered as a gubernatorial candidate because she felt it was a waste of taxpayer money. By contrast, Blagojevich had a platoon of at least twenty state troopers protecting him daily. It was a stark demonstration of the different financial priorities of the two people running for governor. Judy was endorsed by practically every newspaper[128] and every organization within Illinois, but it was just not enough. Money and television commercials would ultimately prevail.

Election Day, November 7, 2006, was surreal for Judy and her family. Judy, Joe, and Joe's wife, Christina, voted at their polling place, Blythe Park School in Riverside, where Joe had attended first through fifth grades. Ironically, this was also the place where Joe learned about voting from Judy when he was a child. She took him there whenever she voted. She believed

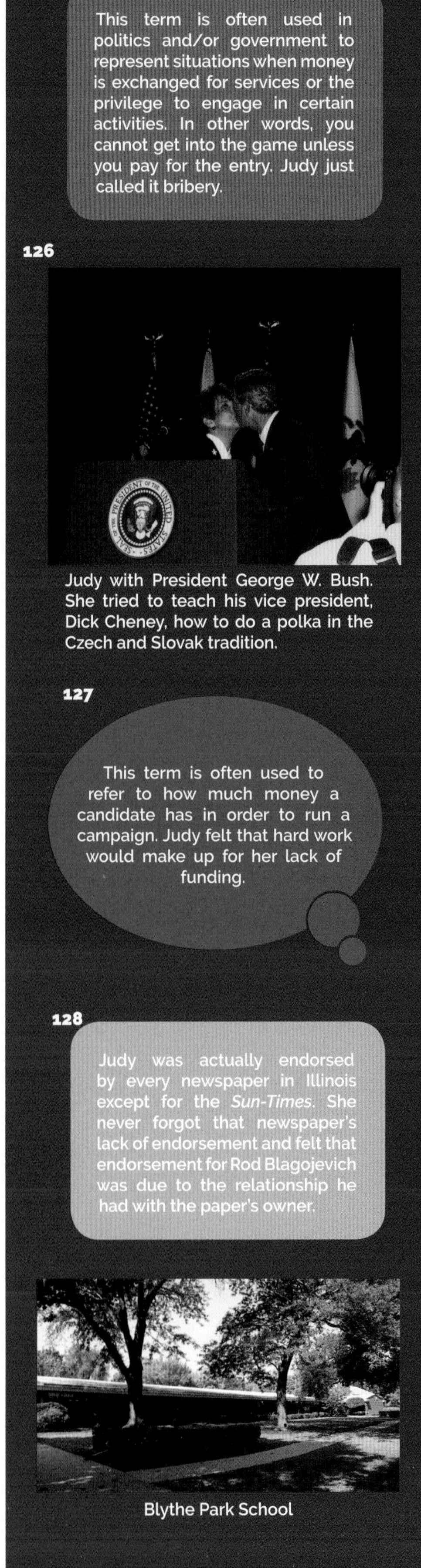

125 This term is often used in politics and/or government to represent situations when money is exchanged for services or the privilege to engage in certain activities. In other words, you cannot get into the game unless you pay for the entry. Judy just called it bribery.

126 Judy with President George W. Bush. She tried to teach his vice president, Dick Cheney, how to do a polka in the Czech and Slovak tradition.

127 This term is often used to refer to how much money a candidate has in order to run a campaign. Judy felt that hard work would make up for her lack of funding.

128 Judy was actually endorsed by every newspaper in Illinois except for the *Sun-Times*. She never forgot that newspaper's lack of endorsement and felt that endorsement for Rod Blagojevich was due to the relationship he had with the paper's owner.

Blythe Park School

STATE OF ILLINOIS

State Board of Elections

TO ALL WHOM IT MAY CONCERN

Pursuant to the provisions of an act of the General Assembly entitled "An Act concerning elections", approved May 11, 1943, we do hereby certify, that at a primary election held in the State of Illinois, on the 21st day of March, 2006, that

JUDY BAAR TOPINKA of RIVERSIDE, ILLINOIS

was duly nominated by the **REPUBLICAN PARTY** as a candidate for the office of **GOVERNOR,** to be voted for at an election to be held in the State of Illinois on the 7th day of November, 2006.

Done at the City of Chicago this 21st day of April 2006.

STATE BOARD OF ELECTIONS

JESSE R. SMART, CHAIRMAN

WANDA L. REDNOUR, VICE CHAIRMAN

PATRICK BRADY, MEMBER

JOHN R. KEITH, MEMBER

BRYAN A. SCHNEIDER, MEMBER

WILLIAM M. MCGUFFAGE, MEMBER

ROBERT J. WALTERS, MEMBER

ALBERT S. PORTER, MEMBER

DANIEL W. WHITE, EXECUTIVE DIRECTOR

The certificate declaring Judy as the Republican candidate for governor after her primary win

Judy on the campaign trail during the governor's race, along with public relations specialist and family friend Roger German

Joe gave Judy a kiss to help her keep her composure as she thanked her supporters on election night.

that parents should take their children with them to vote so their kids could see how the process works. Judy, Joe, and Christina were asked to walk out of the polling place together, arms intertwined in a show of strength, for the news cameras. Joe then accompanied Judy on various errands to get ready for election night and to get down to the hotel campaign headquarters in Chicago. As soon as the polls closed, all the news programs called the election in the favor of Rod Blagojevich. Judy was sad, Joe was sad, and Christina was sad. Judy looked at them and said, "We have to go downstairs and say thank you to everyone."

Judy said her farewells and indicated that she would retire. She hugged practically everyone in that hotel ballroom, and there were hundreds of people. After she was done, Judy looked at Joe and Christina and said, "Well, the room is paid for, do you want to stay the night? It is a nice hotel." Joe replied, "Let's go home to Riverside," and they left without anyone seeing them. Joe's leave from the U.S. Army was almost over, so he and Christina returned to Washington state. He was so sad and angry—sad that his mom lost and angry at the state for voting against her. He wasn't sure he would ever return to Illinois. He just couldn't understand how people could vote for someone who was obviously lacking integrity over someone who had demonstrated over the years that she was honest, fair, and incredibly careful with taxpayers' money. Rod Blagojevich's conduct went against Joe's very fiber as a U.S. Army officer, a military attorney, a federal ethics counselor, and someone who was taught by his mother about common decency toward others.

In the coming months, Judy ensured that the new state treasurer's transition was a good one. The state treasurer-elect, on the other hand, was not so trusting. At their first meeting, he brought his personal lawyer with him. Judy was incensed by this display as she simply wanted to have a heart-to-heart talk with the person taking over the office she had come to love. Judy officially retired and collected her pension, which many in the press corps criticized her for collecting because it was well over the salary she earned while she was treasurer. She did receive more money monthly retired than she made while she was treasurer, but that was because she had been in elected office for so long as both a legislator and as a constitutional officer holder.

What did Judy do in retirement? You know Judy by now—she did many things! She started a radio program called "The Judy Show."[129] It was out of a small, suburban Chicago studio and she interviewed people from many different areas of interest. She did not make any money from doing the show, but it appealed to her journalistic background. She loved to interview people who had great stories to tell. She wrote weekly articles in the local Riverside newspaper, The Landmark, and she did some work for WTTW, the public television station in Chicago, doing political commentary for free. To qualify for a paid position at WTTW, she had to join the Screen Actors Guild,[130] which delighted her because as a member of SAG, she could vote for Screen Actors Guild Award nominations. She continued to support causes she believed in, including generous donations to animal charities. Judy also read a great deal. Over the years, there was not a day that went by that she didn't read several Illinois newspapers. She continued that practice in retirement, giving her a good sense of what was going on in state and local governments.

Being the Illinois Republican Chairman and running for governor had taken a toll on Judy both physically and mentally. On the positive side, Joe was assigned by the U.S. Army to Chicago for civilian schooling at Loyola University from 2007 to 2008. The military often sends its members to civilian schools for advanced education so they can fulfill certain specialty assignments. Joe's next assignment would be in military healthcare in the U.S. Army's Medical Command. Both Joe and Christina were able to spend almost a year with Judy in Riverside. It was overdue family time. Attending Joe's graduation when he received an advanced degree in health law was one of Judy's happiest moments.[131]

Joe and Christina fondly remember how over and over again

The Screen Actors Guild represents approximately 160,000 actors, announcers, broadcast journalists, dancers, DJs, news writers, news editors, program hosts, puppeteers, recording artists, singers, stunt performers, voiceover artists, and other media professionals. SAG-AFTRA members are the faces and voices that entertain and inform America and the world.

In retirement, Judy traveled more and spent quality time with her family and pets.

Judy's son received an LLM in Health Law from Loyola University in Chicago. An LLM is a masters in law degree that gives a lawyer a particular specialization in law.

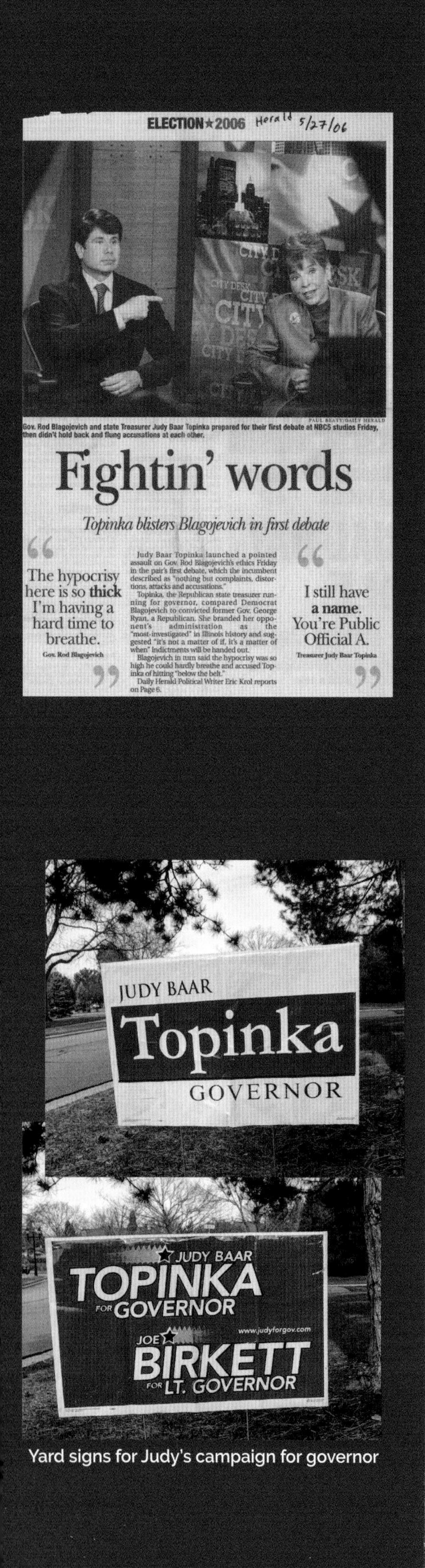

ELECTION★2006 Herald 5/27/06

PAUL BEATY/DAILY HERALD

Gov. Rod Blagojevich and state Treasurer Judy Baar Topinka prepared for their first debate at NBC5 studios Friday, then didn't hold back and flung accusations at each other.

Fightin' words

Topinka blisters Blagojevich in first debate

"The hypocrisy here is so **thick** I'm having a hard time to breathe."
Gov. Rod Blagojevich

Judy Baar Topinka launched a pointed assault on Gov. Rod Blagojevich's ethics Friday in the pair's first debate, which the incumbent described as "nothing but complaints, distortions, attacks and accusations."

Topinka, the Republican state treasurer running for governor, compared Democrat Blagojevich to convicted former Gov. George Ryan, a Republican. She branded her opponent's administration as the "most-investigated" in Illinois history and suggested "it's not a matter of if, it's a matter of when" indictments will be handed out.

Blagojevich in turn said the hypocrisy was so high he could hardly breathe and accused Topinka of hitting "below the belt."

Daily Herald Political Writer Eric Krol reports on Page 6.

"I still have **a name.** You're Public Official A."
Treasurer Judy Baar Topinka

Yard signs for Judy's campaign for governor

people would come up to Judy in restaurants and say: "I voted for you!" She would say, "thank you." She always talked politely to everyone who approached her. Later she would say to her son that people saying they voted for her reminded her of the comments made in France after World War II: "Everyone would always say that they were part of the French resistance against the Nazi occupiers in Vichy France." The problem was that not everyone was part of the French resistance, and the majority of people in Illinois did not vote for Judy or she would have won the election.

In August 2008, just prior to Joe's reassignment to U.S. Army Medical Command at Fort Sam Houston in Texas, Judy told him that her chief of staff when she was state treasurer wanted to meet with her and Joe. Judy was talking about running for another office, but Joe and Christina discouraged it. They both felt it would be bad for her health. During a dinner at The Chew Chew restaurant in Riverside, Illinois, Judy, her former chief of staff, and her son talked about Judy's future. Judy's former chief of staff asked Joe, "I heard you don't support your mother running for comptroller?" Joe said, "That is true." After some discussion, Joe looked to his left in the booth where his mother was sitting. He asked Judy, "What do you want to do, Ma?" Her response, and his reluctant support, would usher in another historic first for Judy and Illinois.

Resources for Further Research

Visit these sites to learn more about...

National political committees:

- Republican National Committee: https://www.gop.com.
- Democratic National Committee: http://www.democraticnationalcommittee.org/home.html.

Major political parties in Illinois:

- Illinois Republican Party: http://illinois.gop.
- Illinois Democratic Party: http://ildems.com.

Smaller political parties in Illinois:

- America First Party of Illinois: http://www.americafirstparty.org/contacts/il.shtml.
- Communist Party of Illinois: http://communistpartyofillinois.tumblr.com.
- Constitution Party of Illinois: http://constitutionpartyil.com.
- Illinois Green Party: http://www.ilgp.org.
- Illinois Libertarian Party: http://www.lpillinois.org/index.php.
- The Unity Party of Illinois: http://www.americanreform.org.

Small political parties nationally:

- American Patriot Party: http://www.pacificwestcom.com/stateparties/ILLINOIS/illinois.html.
- American Reform Party: http://www.americanreform.org.
- Socialist Party of America: http://www.americanreform.org.

Political Media:

- Chicago Tonight (http://chicagotonight.wttw.com/politics) is the WTTW Channel 11 show that Judy was at one time invited to be on as a commentator, though it never worked out. However, she was often a guest on the show.
- Dick Kay is on the radio (http://www.wcpt820.com/dick-kay) on WCPT 820 AM.
- The Screen Actors' Guild is at: http://www.sagaftra.org.
- The Riverside Chamber of Commerce is at: http://riversidechamberofcommerce.com. Judy loved Riverside and all of its businesses, especially its restaurants. She was a particular fan of Aunt Diana's Old Fashioned Fudge and was known to send chocolates and fudge from Aunt Diana's to wherever her son was assigned in the U.S. Army.
- The U.S. Court system has some great information about federal courts and jury service (http://www.uscourts.gov/services-forms/jury-service). The State of Illinois also has great information regarding Illinois courts and jury service (http://www.illinoiscourts.gov.)

Civics Project Ideas and Classroom Learning Activities

government institutions
current and controversial issues
service learning
democratic processes
heritage
compromise
leadership
critical thinking

Chapter 8 Key Concepts:

- Election Process
- Political Campaigns
- Civility
- Integrity

Chapter 8 Classroom Activities (Teacher):

- Discuss with students what a political campaign is. What are typical campaign activities and what is the purpose of a campaign in the election process? Why is it called campaigning? Introduce the concept of tone and positive vs. negative campaign tactics. What are the pros and cons of different campaign approaches? Define civility for your students and ask students for examples of civility in various situations. How can they be more civil to each other and to other people? Why should people be civil to each other?

Chapter 8 Essay Topics (Student):

- If you were governor of Illinois, what would you do on your first day of office?
- GRADE 8: After reading the chapter, write about what you think happened in the campaign for governor between Judy Baar Topinka and Rod Blagojevich. What lessons do you see in the story...about politics and about how to treat people?

United States Court of Appeals
For the Seventh Circuit
219 South Dearborn Street
Chicago, IL 60604
312/435-5810

May 18, 2017

Chambers of
William J. Bauer
Circuit Judge

Dear Reader:

As you have read the chapters of this book about Judy, you have most certainly realized that Judy was different in a great way. She wanted to make things better for everyone in her community and she never gave up.

Sometimes, however, bad things happen to good people; that is why we have a judicial system. The system is designed to ensure that justice is done even under the most trying times. While Judy was a member of the legislative branch and then the executive branch in Illinois, she truly understood the role of the judicial branch in our society and even encouraged her son to become part of that system as an attorney. I encourage you to learn more about the federal and state judiciaries at http://www.uscourts.gov/ and http:/www.illinoiscourts.gov/.

Even after her loss in the race for Illinois Governor, Judy came back fighting, and you will read about her run for Illinois Comptroller in Chapter 9. She campaigned with spirit and style as she had done in the past. I was personally proud of her winning the election and her continued service as a public servant for the good of her state.

As is the law, elected officials must be sworn into their positions. Judy's son swore her in as Comptroller under Illinois law as he was an active duty, military officer at the time. When she was re-elected as Comptroller in 2014, Judy asked me to swear her in, and I was honored by her request.

Unfortunately, she died after the election. I will always wish that I could have fulfilled that duty of swearing her in.

Whether as an elected official, a civil servant, a member of the military, a volunteer, or even a judge, consider pursuing a life in public service as Judy had done. It is a noble duty, and one that I have pursued all my life.

Judy is a role model for me. Judy can be a role model for you.

William J. Bauer

132

The expression "comeback kid" is often used to refer to someone who overcomes a failure and succeeds after trying very hard. Judy worked very hard and made an unlikely comeback when she ran for comptroller.

133

A petition is what a candidate needs to have signed by registered voters in order to file with the Illinois State Board of Elections so that the candidate can be on a ballot. Just because a voter signs the petition does not mean the voter has to vote for the person. It just means that the voter agrees that the person should have a chance to run for a particular office.

134

135

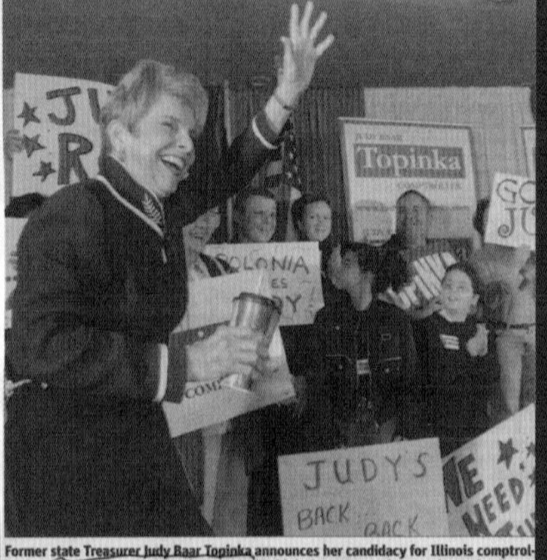
TOPINKA BACK FOR MORE

Former state Treasurer Judy Baar Topinka announces her candidacy for Illinois comptroller Sunday at Ina's restaurant downtown. "I think the state needs a good mooring because there is a floating and a drift," Topinka said recently in a press release. She lost the 2006 gubernatorial race to now-impeached Rod Blagojevich. | AL PODGORSKI–SUN-TIMES

The Comeback Judy[132]

It was August 2008 and Joe was leaving Illinois, driving to his new assignment at Fort Sam Houston in Texas. Judy was sad to see him and her daughter-in-law go. She later told Joe that she often passed the townhouse building that Joe and Christina had rented on Ogden Avenue in Riverside and imagined seeing the two of them days, weeks, and even months later. However, emotions did not get in the way with her circulating petitions[133] to run for the position of Illinois state comptroller.[134] On October 25, 2009, Judy made it official at Ina's Restaurant in downtown Chicago.[135] This was a very low-key announcement compared to previous ones. She even had told her son that there was no need for him to attend.

What is the office of Illinois comptroller that Judy was seeking, and how is it different from the Illinois treasurer's office? Under Section 17 of Article V of the Illinois Constitution, the comptroller maintains the main financial accounts of the state and manages payments into and out of the funds held by the Illinois treasurer. The comptroller signs paychecks to state employees and creditors and also regulates cemeteries under the Cemetery Care Act. Under Section 18 of Article V, the treasurer is responsible for managing the state money. The treasurer is like the state's top banker, and the comptroller is considered the state's chief financial officer.[136] The two offices have different responsibilities but are very similar in that they both deal with the state's financial matters.

Judy never understood why both the comptroller and treasurer offices existed and felt maintaining separate offices was a waste of taxpayers' money. She believed it was just another way the party in power had an extra patronage[137] position to fill with a party loyalist or supporter. She always wanted the two offices to be merged but was continually blocked in her efforts by the speaker of the Illinois House of Representatives, Michael Madigan, who had been speaker since Judy was a legislator.

It was interesting that Judy's announcement that she was

getting back into government came at the same time as another big announcement that foreshadowed Governor Rod Blagojevich's ultimate departure from government. Just a month before Judy's announcement, Governor Blagojevich, who beat Judy in the last election, was arrested on December 9, 2008, and charged with conspiracy to commit mail and wire fraud and solicitation of bribery. The complaint[138] written by the U.S. Attorney in Chicago, who is a representative of the Attorney General of the United States, was backed up by evidence from secret FBI recordings of Governor Blagojevich talking about his attempt to sell President Barack Obama's former Illinois Senate seat in exchange for anything he could get in return. Normally, when a U.S. senator is elected president of the United States, his or her home state will have laws about how the now-vacant Senate seat should be filled by someone else. However, in this case, Governor Blagojevich did not follow Illinois's laws for filling President Obama's Senate seat; rather, he tried to use the seat as a bargaining chip, an act that is both illegal and unethical, and it can lead to corruption in government. In other words, he was using the same "pay-to-play" practices Judy had spoken against over and over during the election for governor.

Judy called her son Joe in Texas and asked him if he had heard the news. He had not, but he wasn't surprised when his mother told him about the arrest. He wondered why the U.S. Attorney had only now taken action? Joe was still angry over the gubernatorial election results from 2006 and felt the U.S. Attorney's actions came more than two years too late.[139] Judy said she was just sad because things could have been different. After talking for a while, both agreed that the entire situation was simply unfortunate for Illinois as a whole.

Judy's campaign for Illinois state comptroller was not well publicized. It was overshadowed by the fury and press coverage the Rod Blagojevich case generated in the press. Four months after the complaint was filed by U.S. Attorney Patrick Fitzgerald, Blagojevich was indicted by a grand jury. The U.S. Attorney's office had evidence going all the way back

136 Many in Illinois, including the current Illinois Speaker of the House of Representatives, Mike Madigan, believe that the two offices should remain separate as a result of a 1965 scandal involving the then-auditor, Republican Orville Hodge. Hodge spent six years in prison for corruption and embezzlement of state funds, which he used to buy two private jets, several new cars, property in Florida, and a lake house in Springfield. Delegates to Illinois's last Constitutional Convention in 1970, which included Mr. Madigan, felt that the treasurer should invest money and the comptroller should handle day-to-day financial operations in order to maintain separation. Judy felt that technology, greater openness in government, and the establishment of a statewide auditor allowed for the two positions to be combined at incredible savings to taxpayers.

137 Patronage means giving jobs to people based on politics; for example, rewarding a person who helped you in your campaign with a government job if you win the election. In 1990, the U.S. Supreme Court stated in the case Rutan v. Republican Party of Illinois that, with few exceptions, hiring, firing, promoting, and transferring state workers cannot be based on politics. However, many politicians and government leaders keep an inner circle of staff who they consider to be among the exceptions to the Supreme Court's decision.

138 A complaint is different than an indictment. A complaint is normally approved by a judge based on probable cause, which is a term that commonly refers to having enough information that something probably happened based on evidence collected. In the case of Rod Blagojevich, a complaint was needed in order to arrest him and stop his further criminal conduct. A complaint is almost always followed by an indictment. Judy's son was consistently amazed that things happened so quickly in 2008 with President Obama's Senate seat involved, but that there was no such sense of urgency during the campaign for governor, when it mattered most to Judy.

to 2002, even before Rod Blagojevich was governor, to support its case. In all, the U.S. Attorney's accusation contained sixteen felony counts. A felony is the most serious of charges that can be made against a person. The charges against Blagojevich included complicated crimes like racketeering conspiracy, wire fraud, extortion conspiracy, attempted extortion, and making false statements to federal agents. Another surprising allegation in the indictment was that Rod Blagojevich unsuccessfully tried to extort (to obtain something by force, threats, or other unfair means) campaign funds from Rahm Emanuel, who would later become President Barack Obama's chief of staff and then mayor of Chicago.

Not to be outdone by the U.S. Attorney in Chicago and a federal grand jury, the Illinois General Assembly took action against Rod Blagojevich in early 2009. On January 8, 2009, the Illinois House of Representatives voted 114–1 (with three abstentions) to impeach[140] Blagojevich. The charges brought by the House focused on Blagojevich's alleged abuses of power as well as his attempts to sell appointments that he could make as governor and legislative authorizations and/or vetoes. One of the claims was the alleged attempt to sell the appointment to the United States Senate seat vacated by the resignation of Barack Obama when he became President of the United States. Blagojevich was removed from office and prohibited from ever holding public office in the state of Illinois again by two separate and unanimous votes of 59–0 by the Illinois Senate on January 29, 2009. Blagojevich's lieutenant governor, Patrick Quinn, who had held the office of Illinois state treasurer before Judy, became governor of Illinois.

With so much attention on Rod Blagojevich, not many people took much notice of Judy's return to politics—nor did they realize why she pursued this office. She was angry about what was happening to her beloved state of Illinois. "I take no satisfaction in having been right, because it meant that so many in the state have been wronged," Topinka said to one newspaper, referring to the troubles that led to Blagojevich's indictment and impeachment. Judy had told Joe that she

139

A picture of Judy and Joe after she announced her candidacy for a second term as Illinois comptroller in 2013. Judy often told people that her son was angrier at her loss for governor than she was, but in the end her son was more concerned by what the election and politics had done to her health.

HR0005 -3- LRB096 04262 RCE 14308 r

thereby impeached Governor Rod R. Blagojevich; and

WHEREAS, The House of Representatives of the Ninety-Sixth General Assembly chooses to reaffirm the actions taken by the House of Representatives of the Ninety-Fifth General Assembly in its adoption of House Resolution 1671; therefore, be it

RESOLVED, BY THE HOUSE OF REPRESENTATIVES OF THE NINETY-SIXTH GENERAL ASSEMBLY OF THE STATE OF ILLINOIS, that Rod R. Blagojevich, Governor of the State of Illinois, is impeached for cause and that the following article of impeachment be exhibited to the Senate for trial as provided in the Illinois Constitution so that the Senate may do justice according to law:

ARTICLE OF IMPEACHMENT EXHIBITED BY THE HOUSE OF REPRESENTATIVES IN THE NAME OF ITSELF AND THE PEOPLE OF THE STATE OF ILLINOIS AGAINST ROD R. BLAGOJEVICH, GOVERNOR OF THE STATE OF ILLINOIS, IN MAINTENANCE OF THE IMPEACHMENT OF HIM FOR CAUSE.

ARTICLE ONE

Based on the totality of the evidence contained in the

140

Impeachment in Illinois is described in Section 14 of Article IV of the Illinois Constitution. The provision specifically states that "[t]he House of Representatives has the sole power to conduct legislative investigations to determine the existence of cause for impeachment and, by the vote of a majority of the members elected, to impeach Executive and Judicial officers. Impeachments shall be tried by the Senate. When sitting for that purpose, Senators shall be upon oath, or affirmation, to do justice according to law. If the Governor is tried, the Chief Justice of the Supreme Court shall preside. No person shall be convicted without the concurrence of two-thirds of the Senators elected. Judgment shall not extend beyond removal from office and disqualification to hold any public office of this State. An impeached officer, whether convicted or acquitted, shall be liable to prosecution, trial, judgment and punishment according to law." Above is a page from the Illinois House Resolution that brought articles of impeachment against Blagojevich.

never wanted to say "I told you so." She just wanted to make things better.[141] Judy's desire to run for comptroller was authentic, and she was impassioned to act by what she had seen happen to Illinois after leaving the treasurer's office.

Judy was already working hard to get elected, but something occurred in her life that further made her want to make things better. On March 9, 2010, she became a grandmother, a babi, and most likely started to think about the future for her granddaughter. Her son had a babi, Judy had a babi, and now she was a babi. The news of the birth of Alexandra Faith Baar Topinka at Wilford Hall Medical Center on the Lackland Air Force Base outside San Antonio, Texas, excited Judy to no end. Everywhere she went, she told people: "I am a babi! I am a babi!" Her Czech heritage and her love of her new granddaughter brought great energy to her pursuit of this new office.

On November 7, 2010, Judy won the election and made her "comeback" to Illinois government, adding this new achievement to her life's assortment of accomplishments. Judy Baar Topinka was the first person in Illinois elected to two constitutional offices and the only person, man or woman, to hold both top financial offices in Illinois.

Judy was sworn in at the Prairie State Convention Center in Springfield on January 10, 2011. Every Illinois constitutional office holder gets to choose who will swear them in, and Judy had been wanting her son, Joe, to swear her in for years. Each time she was up on stage at the Prairie State Convention Center as Illinois State Treasurer, Joe was in uniform and was prevented by law as a military officer from swearing her in while in uniform. This time, Joe did not wear his uniform. He had been made a Special Officer under Illinois law, authorizing him to swear his mother into office.[142] He worked for weeks on memorizing the oath so that he could say it by heart. Judy held her left hand on the Bible given to her by her parents in 1960 and raised her right hand. Halfway through the oath, she interrupted her son asking him whether the oath was a little too long. Joe's memory practically went blank at the

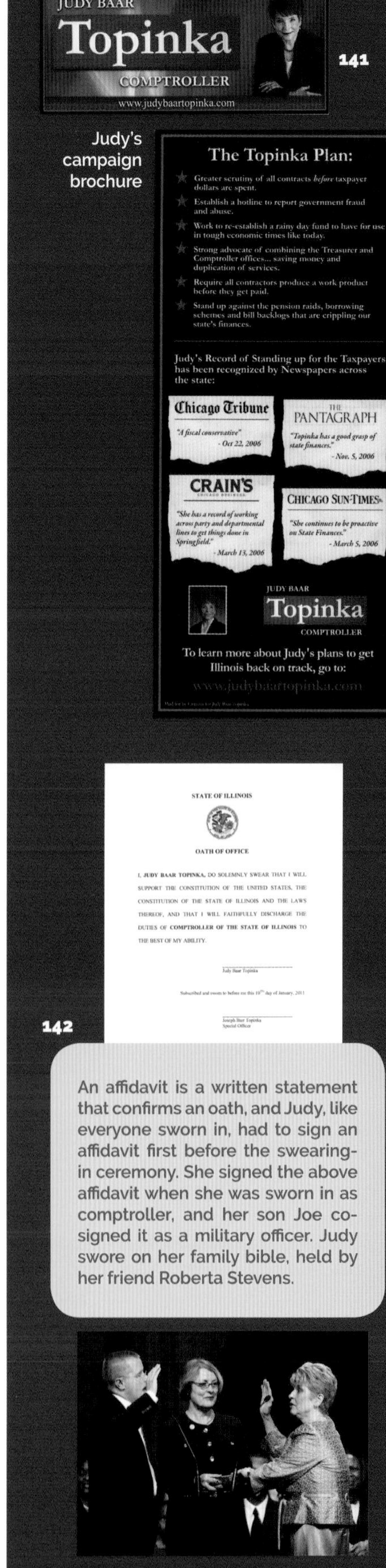

JUDY BAAR
Topinka
COMPTROLLER
www.judybaartopinka.com
141
The Topinka Plan:
Greater scrutiny of all contracts *before* taxpayer dollars are spent.
Establish a hotline to report government fraud and abuse.
Work to re-establish a rainy day fund to have for use in tough economic times like today.
Strong advocate of combining the Treasurer and Comptroller offices... saving money and duplication of services.
Require all contractors produce a work product before they get paid.
Stand up against the pension raids, borrowing schemes and bill backlogs that are crippling our state's finances.
Judy's Record of Standing up for the Taxpayers has been recognized by Newspapers across the state:
Chicago Tribune
"A fiscal conservative" - Oct 22, 2006
THE PANTAGRAPH
"Topinka has a good grasp of state finances." - Nov. 5, 2006
CRAIN'S
"She has a record of working across party and departmental lines to get things done in Springfield." - March 13, 2006
CHICAGO SUN-TIMES
"She continues to be proactive on State Finances." - March 5, 2006
JUDY BAAR
Topinka
COMPTROLLER
To learn more about Judy's plans to get Illinois back on track, go to:
www.judybaartopinka.com

Judy's campaign brochure

142

STATE OF ILLINOIS

OATH OF OFFICE

I, **JUDY BAAR TOPINKA,** DO SOLEMNLY SWEAR THAT I WILL SUPPORT THE CONSTITUTION OF THE UNITED STATES, THE CONSTITUTION OF THE STATE OF ILLINOIS AND THE LAWS THEREOF, AND THAT I WILL FAITHFULLY DISCHARGE THE DUTIES OF **COMPTROLLER OF THE STATE OF ILLINOIS** TO THE BEST OF MY ABILITY.

Judy Baar Topinka

Subscribed and sworn to before me this 10th day of January, 2011

Joseph Baar Topinka
Special Officer

An affidavit is a written statement that confirms an oath, and Judy, like everyone sworn in, had to sign an affidavit first before the swearing-in ceremony. She signed the above affidavit when she was sworn in as comptroller, and her son Joe co-signed it as a military officer. Judy swore on her family bible, held by her friend Roberta Stevens.

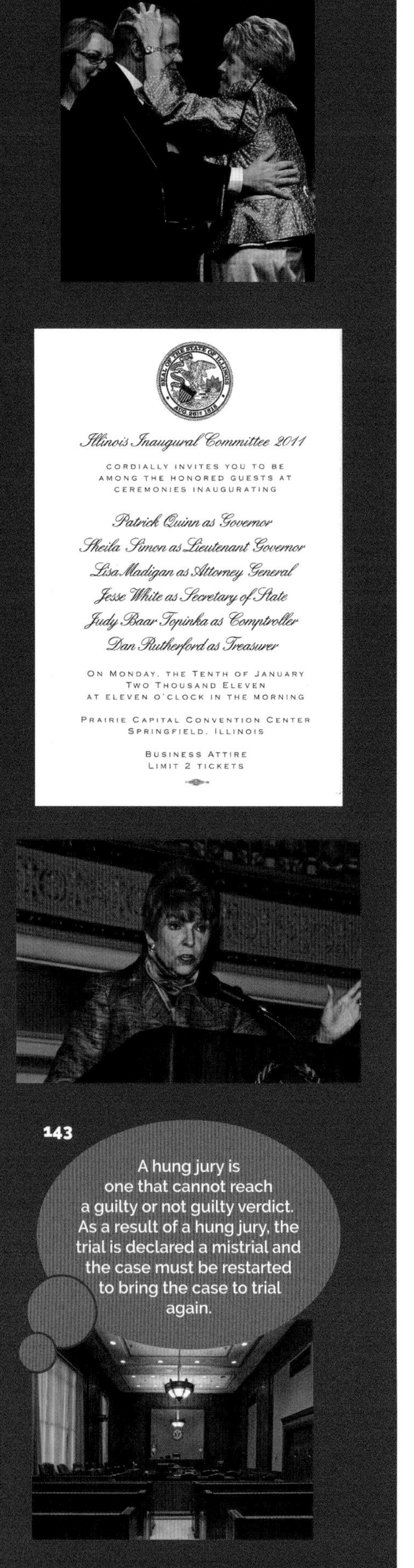

Illinois Inaugural Committee 2011

CORDIALLY INVITES YOU TO BE AMONG THE HONORED GUESTS AT CEREMONIES INAUGURATING

Patrick Quinn as Governor
Sheila Simon as Lieutenant Governor
Lisa Madigan as Attorney General
Jesse White as Secretary of State
Judy Baar Topinka as Comptroller
Dan Rutherford as Treasurer

ON MONDAY, THE TENTH OF JANUARY
TWO THOUSAND ELEVEN
AT ELEVEN O'CLOCK IN THE MORNING

PRAIRIE CAPITAL CONVENTION CENTER
SPRINGFIELD, ILLINOIS

BUSINESS ATTIRE
LIMIT 2 TICKETS

distraction, but he was able to get Judy to finish the oath. Everyone laughed. Then Judy rubbed Joe's short hair as only a mom could do—in front of a packed convention center with thousands of people laughing—and then kissed her son on the cheek. It would be the last time Judy and her son would ever go through such a ceremony.

Judy's speech that day had a flair that had come to be expected by the people of Illinois from Judy Baar Topinka. They could always count on humor wrapped with a little skepticism in delivering a powerful and positive message about Illinois's future. She thanked Joe for swearing her in and then she told the audience, "Well, let me tell you what I am thinking. I am thinking it is time to put aside the petty bickering and partisan fights, roll up our sleeves, and turn this state around. State government has gotten out of touch and out of control." The audience clapped excitedly and it laughed because it was obvious that Judy was making a reference to the campaign refrain then-Governor Rod Blagojevich had made repeatedly in television and radio campaign commercials around the state and especially in the Chicago metropolitan market.

Ironically, months before, on August 17, 2010, Blagojevich had been convicted of one of the twenty-four federal charges by a federal jury. The jury was hung[143] on the twenty-three other charges. Blagojevich was retried, which meant his case began anew, finally ending on June 27, 2011. He was found guilty of seventeen of the twenty remaining charges. Federal prosecutors reduced the number of charges against him after the first trial failed to convict him. Being found guilty meant he would be going to prison or "serving time."

While Blagojevich began serving time as a federal convict, Judy was making the Illinois comptroller's office more efficient through the use of technology and by lowering the cost of operating the office. She began to push for both the offices of treasurer and comptroller to be combined in order to save taxpayers $12 million dollars annually. Unfortunately, such efforts were blocked. She eliminated all the paper bills and files by computerizing everything. There used to literally be a pile of

143 A hung jury is one that cannot reach a guilty or not guilty verdict. As a result of a hung jury, the trial is declared a mistrial and the case must be restarted to bring the case to trial again.

bills and files, she'd marvel. Most importantly, she was ensuring that the people that were owed money by the State of Illinois were paid as quickly as possible. When she arrived, those who were owed money previously had to wait anywhere from six months to more than one year to be paid by the state.

Judy used to get frustrated that the Illinois General Assembly would only appropriate funds for half a year and then, when the state went through what it had budgeted, bills would increase and she would have to "slow walk" the payments. In other words, she would delay making payments for as long as she could legally do so. She once wrote, "It is quite magical how our office works…trying to pay bills with little to no money and keep the floodgates from popping." Judy told her son that she tried so hard to ensure that small, non-profit social organizations received payment before larger organizations that could weather the lack of income longer. Her concern was that these social organizations provided money, services, and support to less fortunate people in Illinois like the sick, disabled, and the abused. Without state money, they would shut down and thousands of people would be left without support; it would quite literally undermine the social support structure in Illinois. People loved her for caring as she did. Big companies such as medical insurance companies were less pleased.

Judy had a style all her own, especially when it came to the wonderful causes she pursued and supported. She was a morale builder with her employees, a booster of Illinois history, and an enthusiastic promoter of Illinois businesses that produced products for the country and the world. She bought posters at estate sales she visited around the state to liven up the drab walls of the Adams Building where many of her employees worked in Springfield. She published a book about Illinois cemeteries[144] designed to teach kids where famous people are buried in the state. She started the Comptroller's Critters Program to find homes for stray animals and reduce the amount of money the state spent dealing with the animals. And Judy continued her spring tradition of Eli's Cheesecake Day, which she started in 1993.[145] She loved Eli's Cheesecake,

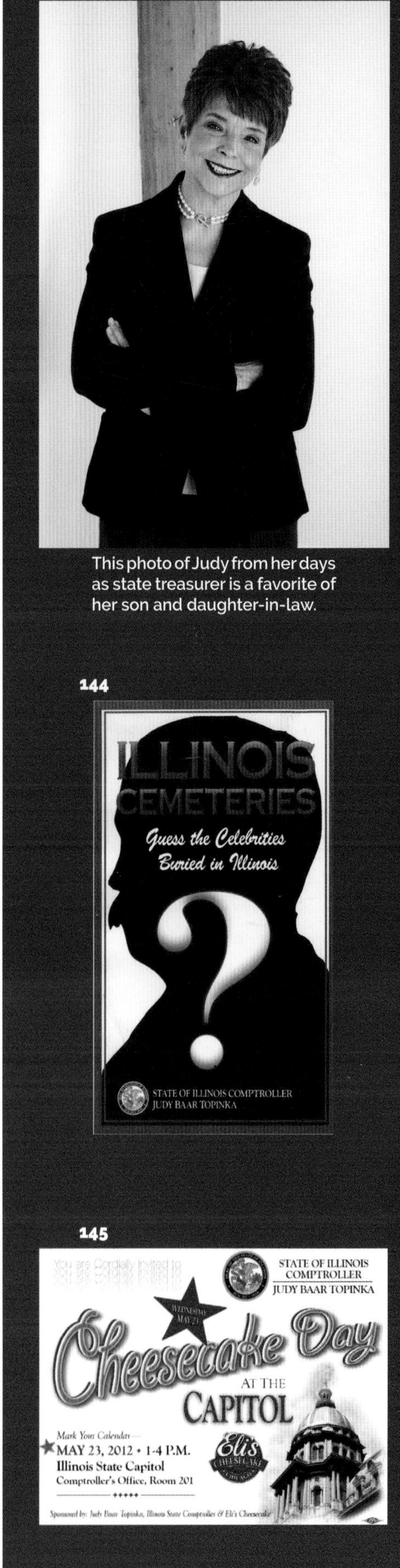

This photo of Judy from her days as state treasurer is a favorite of her son and daughter-in-law.

144

145

just as she loved to support Illinois products, especially its food, like hot dogs, pizza, and candy. If a product was from Illinois like Tootsie Roll candy or Vienna beef hot dogs, or even the Springfield horseshoe sandwich, she endorsed it and took every opportunity to brag about it to the world.

Judy loved being comptroller and she loved the people she served. She announced that she would run for a second term as Illinois comptroller on September 17, 2013. Judy traveled around the state on September 17 and 18 with Joe, who was on military leave, making the announcement. They began at the famous Billy Goat Tavern in Chicago and ended in Southern Illinois after stops in Rockford, Peoria, Springfield, Quincy, and Edwardsville, to name a few. Military ethics regulations prohibited Joe from being at the podium with his mom during the announcement, but he was in the audience at each location being supportive as always.

This campaign for comptroller, however, would be more visible than the last one because the daughter of the late Senator Paul Simon,[146] Sheila Simon, was in the race against Judy. Sheila Simon was a former Illinois Lieutenant Governor. She personally attacked Judy, especially in 2014, for trying to help Joe get a job when he retired from the U.S. Army in late March. As a result of these personal attacks, Joe stopped looking for work in Illinois. He also did not campaign for Judy after his military retirement to avoid drawing more public criticism against his mother. The campaign became very ugly and reminiscent of Judy's run for governor. Judy won the election on November 7, 2014, but the election had taken its toll on her health. She was tired and in pain.

Joe recalled that on September 18, 2013, when Judy was in Southern Illinois exiting her campaign bus to make a campaign speech at a local ice cream shop, Judy fell, face first, off the narrow steps onto the gravel paved parking lot of the business. Joe witnessed this scene in horror. Judy of course got up and dusted herself off as she always did, but she was, in fact, in pain. That event would foreshadow an incredibly negative and stressful political campaign and Judy's untimely death in 2014.

Some of Illinois' most famous foods

The Billy Goat Tavern has been a Chicago landmark since 1934.

146

Senator Paul Simon was from Southern Illinois. He served in the United States House of Representatives from 1975 to 1985 and the United States Senate from 1985 to 1997. He also ran for president in 1998. Judy looked up to Paul Simon as a role model for a statesman and governmental leader. His trademark was a bow tie, and Judy received this one from Sen. Simon's widow after his death.

Resources for Further Research

Visit these sites to learn more about:

- The Illinois Constitution: http://www.ilga.gov/commission/lrb/conmain.htm.
- The Illinois Treasurer's Office: http://www.illinoistreasurer.gov.
- The Illinois Comptroller's Office: http://illinoiscomptroller.gov.
- The Illinois Auditor General's Office: http://www.auditor.illinois.gov.

After his political career, Senator Paul Simon founded the Public Policy Institute at Southern Illinois University in Carbondale, a great source of information about public policy in Illinois, the United States, and the world. It is now named after him: http://paulsimoninstitute.siu.edu/index.php.

You can try Judy Baar Topinka's favorite cheesecake at Eli's Cheesecake World at 6701 W. Forest Preserve Drive, Chicago, IL 60034 (http://www.elicheesecake.com).

Judy loved products from Illinois! State Gifts U.S.A. (http://www.stategiftsusa.com/made-in-illinois) has a list of some wonderful products from Illinois.

Civics Project Ideas and Classroom Learning Activities

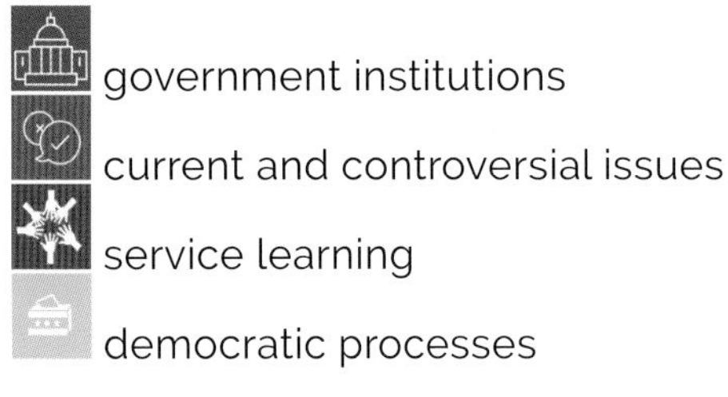

- government institutions
- current and controversial issues
- service learning
- democratic processes
- heritage
- compromise
- leadership
- critical thinking

Chapter 9 Key Concepts:

- Sacrifice
- Perseverance
- Balance
- Responsibility
- Maturity

Chapter 9 Classroom Activities (Teacher):

- Review with your students the difference between the Illinois Treasurer and the Illinois Comptroller. Get a copy of the Illinois Constitution of 1970 and read the descriptions of both offices. Why are there two offices? What are the pros and cons of combining the offices as Judy Baar Topinka wanted?

- Discuss with your students the importance of perseverance. Ask for examples of times when they didn't give up. How did they feel during the process? After? Was the outcome for them enduring?

- Have students consider the concept of balance in life? How does it relate to them now? How do they imagine it is important as they go through life?

Chapter 9 Essay Topics (Student):

- Write about which position you would rather have, Illinois Treasurer or Illinois Comptroller. Which one has more influence? Which one do you think is more important to the State of Illinois?

- GRADE 8: Do you think the Illinois Constitution of 1970 should be rewritten? Write about how you would change the current Illinois Constitution and make it better for everyone.

The Judy Philosophy. Can it Apply to You?

In the early morning of December 10, 2014, Joe found himself running to MacNeal Memorial Hospital in Berwyn. It was the same hospital where he was born to Judy Baar Topinka almost half a century earlier. Now he was running to see his mother, who would soon die in front of his eyes. Judy had a stroke the day before, and he had flown into town immediately. He was at Judy's Riverside house preparing to visit her when he received a phone call from a member of her staff staying that his mom was having a seizure. He hadn't been able to find Judy's car keys to drive there, so he ran to the hospital instead. And as he ran and ran, he cried out loud, saying to himself, "Please do not let this be it. Please do not let her die. It is not the right time." But Judy Baar Topinka died shortly after Joe arrived at the hospital. Joe lost his best friend and his mother that morning. He didn't understand how she could die right then; he didn't believe it was her time to leave.

There is never a right time for death—especially for someone like Judy, who was loved by so many, including her son, daughter-in-law, and granddaughter. To lots of people, Judy was like Margaret "Maggie" Brown[147] (also known as "The Unsinkable Molly Brown") in that she was expected to always be around no matter the issue or the obstacle. However, everyone dies, and no one can predict when that day will come. When it does, though, it's important to reflect on the person's life and learn from it. Judy, her ideas, her actions, and her way with others and in office give us a lot to consider. One of Judy's good friends told Joe months later that his mom was amazing because it was as if she had lived by a "philosophy of life." That philosophy guided her in focusing on good government, civility, perseverance, balance, integrity, heritage, and most of all, fighting for things that mattered most to her and her constituents.

147 Margaret Brown is remembered for being one of the survivors of the RMS Titanic in Lifeboat No. 6, and who allegedly encouraged the crew of the lifeboat to go back to look for survivors of the ship after it sank in 1912. She received the name "The Unsinkable Molly Brown" after her death and after a musical and 1964 film gave her the nickname. Judy was fascinated by the history of the RMS Titanic and read many books about the eyewitness accounts of the tragedy.

Judy with Margaret Thatcher, the first woman to serve as prime minister of the United Kingdom

Judy and Chicago Mayor Rahm Emanuel

Judy during her run for governor. Her daughter-in-law, Christina (far right) often came to events as Joe was on active duty in Washington state.

Judy at the Lincoln Memorial in Washington, D.C. in 2004. The Lincoln and Jefferson memorials were her favorites in D.C. because of the great quotes by both leaders inscribed into their walls.

Good Government Is Good Management and Leadership

What is good government? People have been asking this question for centuries. Abraham Lincoln, in his Gettysburg Address, referred to a "[g]overnment of the people, by the people, for the people..." but he did not mention how such a government is managed properly. If good government is for the people, by the people, and of the people, it definitely needs good managers and good leaders. Judy tried hard to be not just a politician but a manager and leader as well.

Not everyone is a good manager and not everyone is a good leader. Sometimes, though, a person is a good manager and a good leader at the same time, and such a combination can result in a person doing great things in public office. Judy realized that being the treasurer, comptroller, and—if she won—the governor, required the ability to manage others, to be the boss responsible for employees and accountable to customers, the citizens of Illinois. She also understood that others would be watching her as a leader, looking to her as a role model. Judy would often say "you can talk the talk but you must walk the walk." In other words, actions speak more than words, and people would judge her as leader by what she did more than what she said.

An elected official in government needs a good formal education, meaningful life experiences, and talent. They also need to really love the people they represent. Judy worked hard to learn as much as she could growing up, she had years of incredible experiences as a reporter and a mother, and she had the talent of being a good listener of the people in her community. She had the additional skill of being able to take what she had heard and make change through legislation, policy, decisions, and innovative ideas. Good government should work for the people. Judy made it her responsibility to listen to what the people wanted, and then she worked to find a way to make something happen for them and to make the state better. Judy knew that not everyone would like her and what she did, but she had a responsibility to the office and she took an oath to ensure that she did the job correctly for the state.

Judy Baar Topinka's greatest honor was being a public servant. Being a public servant was not a cliché or overused expression to her; it was a way of life that she lived until her death in office.[148] What does being a public servant mean to you? How do you and how can you serve those around you? What role in government might you be suited for? How would you like to make the future better? What values do you think make for a good manager or leader in government, business, or life? It was always Judy's hope that she would inspire others to run for public office and lead and manage for the good of the state and the country. Do you think you could be a good governor or president of the United States? Run with the idea and make it happen!

Civility, Protocol, and Compromise

Civility in its basic form is about formal politeness or courtesy. Judy was a great reader of history, especially Illinois history. Illinois's history has been plagued by disputes, distrust, fraud, and lies. Judy always looked up to people like Abraham Lincoln, Paul Simon, and Ronald Reagan because they were Illinois politicians who practiced civility toward others, even toward their enemies. They had good manners and were polite to others, which is just part of being a good person in life. Judy believed manners were so important and part of a common practice of how people treat each other. That common practice is called protocol, and Judy was a true believer of protocol in dealing with people, especially superiors and subordinates. She would tell people to call her Judy on the streets of Chicago, Rockford, Carbondale, Peoria, or even under the capitol rotunda in Springfield,[149] but once in a formal meeting, she would expect to be addressed as Representative, Senator, Madame Treasurer, or Madame Comptroller. At the very least, she expected to be addressed with the polite courtesy of Ma'am.

Judy frequently reminded Joe that manners were the key to civility and, through civility, people could come together to create compromises for the good of the community, the state, or the country. There was an order to how people dealt with

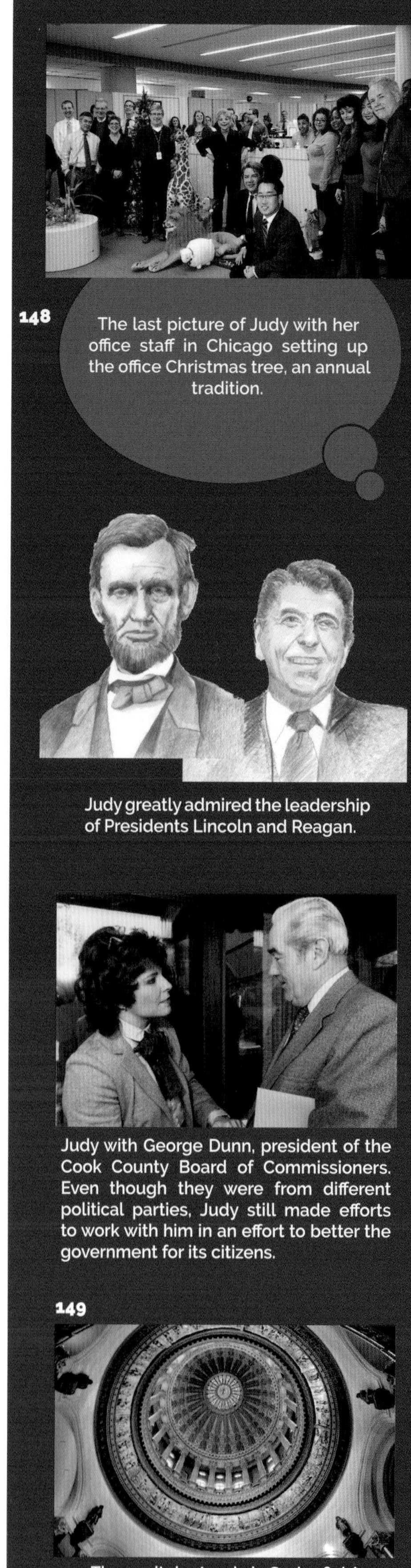

148 The last picture of Judy with her office staff in Chicago setting up the office Christmas tree, an annual tradition.

Judy greatly admired the leadership of Presidents Lincoln and Reagan.

Judy with George Dunn, president of the Cook County Board of Commissioners. Even though they were from different political parties, Judy still made efforts to work with him in an effort to better the government for its citizens.

149 The capitol rotunda in Springfield

each other in business, government, and just life in general, and she expected people to follow it. For example, when Judy was attending her son's swearing-in ceremony at the U.S. Supreme Court in 2003, she was introduced to Justice Ruth Bader Ginsburg[150] by the clerk of the Supreme Court before her son's superior, a two-star general, was introduced to her. By rules of protocol, Judy was the equivalent to a three- or four-star general. When her son was embarrassed because his superior officer was unexpectedly denied a first introduction with a Supreme Court justice (the general did not know about Judy's position beyond being a parent of one of his officers), Judy lectured Joe about the rules of protocol and additionally noted that "[I] control more money and influence more people than your general ever will and that is why there is protocol!"

It was through protocol that Judy was able to deal with people she would not otherwise care to deal with and come up with agreements for the good of the state and her constituents. She did not have to like everyone to work with them but, through appropriate conduct towards all, she was able to create opportunities for both sides to agree and compromise. Compromise is the art of getting along with people and coming up with ways to agree to solve problems for the betterment of all. In business, it is often called "win-win." For Judy, it was just about getting everyone to agree to what made common sense. Illinois is a large state, and people from DeKalb have different interests than people from Carbondale, and beliefs in Champaign-Urbana do not always "play in Peoria."[151] Judy lived by the spirit of compromise and she achieved many compromises through just being civil to other people from different parts of the state, and those compromises led to solutions to problems facing people from Rockford to Cairo and from Taylorsville to Quincy.

How is compromise a good thing in government, business, and daily life? How do you work with others to solve disagreements? Can you think of additional ways to improve your ability to compromise? Do good manners and protocol have a role in your conduct? How can you increase your own

150

Judy looked up to Justice Ginsburg as a woman and as a great thinker. She admired the fact that a woman with such small, physical stature and such shy demeanor could write such incredible opinions.

Judy with President George H. W. Bush

151

"Will it play in Peoria?" was a saying that Judy used often but many people have used this saying for years to question whether an idea will be popular in the United States. Peoria was always seen as a typical American city. If something was popular in Peoria, Illinois, it probably would be popular elsewhere in the United States.

level of civility? Sometimes being nice to others is what life is really all about.

Perseverance

Perseverance means doing something despite great difficulty. It means lasting, enduring, sticking with it, or overcoming the odds. As her story shows, Judy never gave up, even in the face of loss. For example, she persevered during an election for governor despite a lack of money and most probably a lack of support from her own political party. She worked harder than her opponent, in part, by traveling to practically every county in the state of Illinois, while her opponent rarely left Chicago. On election night, as Judy and her family were driving to the hotel for her to make a concession speech to Rod Blagojevich, her campaign manager said out loud, "Judy, you did everything right." He knew it, she knew it, everyone knew it. She lost with honor and she persevered. It was hard, but four years later, Judy was back in office doing the people's work and Blagojevich was on his way to federal confinement in disgrace.

Judy told Joe all his life that "the true test of a person comes when he is slapped down and whether he gets up and fights on. You never give up and when you fail, come back and come back fighting." She lost the race for governor of Illinois, but that did not stop her...she persevered.

Have you ever had an experience where you just felt you could not do something? Did you ever want to just give up? What did you do and why? The next time something feels too tough, how can you think differently about the situation? What things could you do to give yourself the boost needed to persevere? Judy would say to many that "there is no can't in life." You can, if you just do not give up.

Balance

In life, balance is about having a variety of different interests and not putting all of your energy excessively into just one activity. Living like that can be stressful, overwhelming, and sometimes outright boring. It can also lead to disappointment,

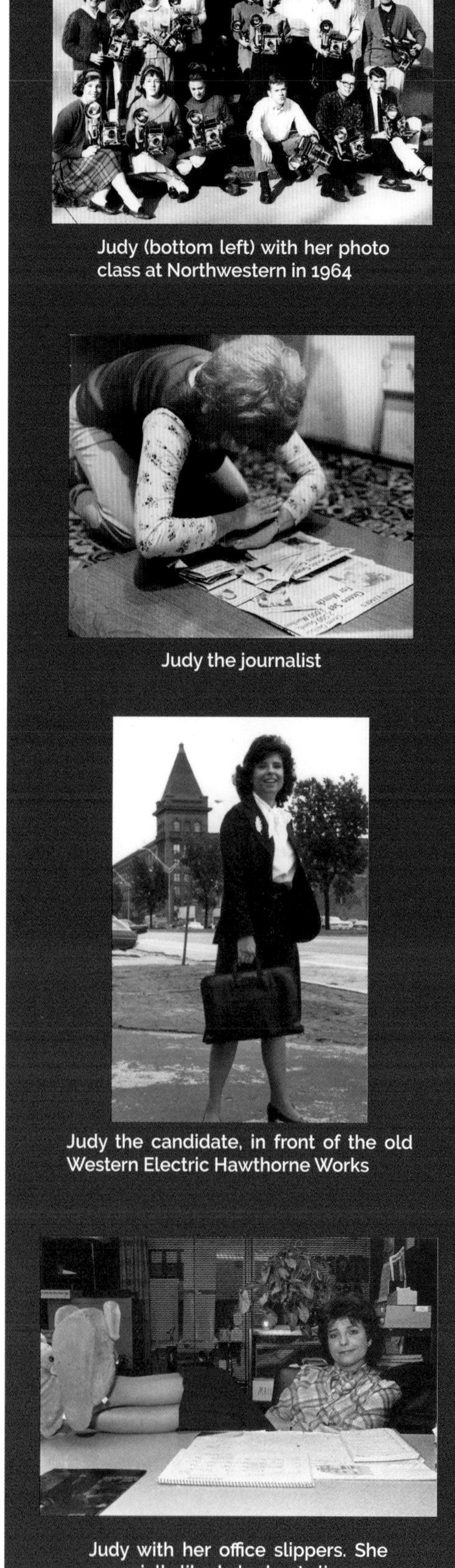

Judy (bottom left) with her photo class at Northwestern in 1964

Judy the journalist

Judy the candidate, in front of the old Western Electric Hawthorne Works

Judy with her office slippers. She especially liked elephant slippers.

Judy and First Lady Barbara Bush

Judy with Sarah, Duchess of York, a former member of the British royal family

Judy met Academy Award-winning actress Shirley MacLaine. People often said the two looked alike!

Judy loved to travel. Here are some of her passports and a brochure of Westminster Abbey in London.

in the event your life changes unexpectedly and that one activity you spent so much energy on pursuing becomes one you can't do anymore. Most of all, it can be unhealthy. After Joe entered active duty in the U.S. Army, Judy's role as his mom drastically changed. She realized that she needed to bring some balance to her life now that Joe was closer to the Arctic Ocean in Alaska than he was to Lake Michigan in Illinois and to her. Judy sometimes was so consumed with her work and spending more time helping others than she did for herself or her family. She needed to have interests that balanced her very full schedule of government work and she began pursuing them. Having a balance of activities and interests can lead to lots of great and different experiences no matter what unexpected changes life may bring in the future.

Judy loved the performing arts—plays, operettas, operas, the symphony—all of it. When Joe came home on military leave, the two of them would attend some performance in Chicago. She loved the Lyric Opera of Chicago and she really enjoyed attending opening night. She relished the Chicago Symphony Orchestra and adored its late music director, Sir George Solti. Appreciating the performing arts in Chicago was very expensive, so she also found less costly ways to enjoy them, such as going to performances at local community colleges, high schools, and theatrical troops based in the suburbs of Chicago, such as the one in which her parents met in Riverside. It was not uncommon for a person to be sitting next to the senior financial officer of the state in a local high school auditorium watching a play and cheering on the young kids and their performances.

Judy also found balance going to estate sales, and she sought them out in all corners of the state. She found treasures that others no longer valued and gave them a home in her museum-like house of items from around the world that were purchased from all around Illinois. Joe liked to say that Judy was a patrician at heart but a plebeian at the pocket book. Like the patrician class of ancient Rome, Judy loved beautiful things and culture in any form, but she was never wealthy, so she was in fact more like a commoner in ancient Rome, known as a plebeian. Often at these estate sales, Judy rescued Czech and Slovak books and artifacts for the University of Chicago's Slavic and East European Collections, or she salvaged military items from veterans and their families and donated them to the Pritzker Museum and Military Library.

Do you ever feel that you're doing the same thing over and over again, and that alone is making you a bit unhappy? Do you often play too much and then have no time to prepare for school, and your grades suffer? Do you ever want to explore other subjects or start a hobby or learn to do something new? Can you think of anything you're doing too much of or spending too much time on? What are some ways to balance that out?

There are so many amazing things to see, do, and experience in the world. Pursue them, but do not do so in excess. Judy loved Greek history and she especially liked reading about the Greek philosophers like Socrates, Plato, and Aristotle. Socrates had a belief that a person "must know how to choose the mean[152] and avoid the extremes on either side, as far as possible." That is great advice from a very wise man and advice that Judy tried but was not always successful in following.

Integrity

Integrity is a quality of wholeness and honesty, of words and deeds matching one's values and moral principles. Judy Baar Topinka was a truthful person. In light of recent political campaigns at the local, state, and national levels, many people cannot believe that a politician can be honest, but Judy truly was honest. She believed that you are only as good as the trust that others have in you. Once you break your word or lie, you never really get treated in the same way again, because people don't know if they can trust you. Judy understood how important her word was to others.

Some people like to think of trust as a relationship "bank account," and this was a concept Judy followed without ever realizing it. You invest in relationships by making valuable deposits through acts of trust, reliability, and responsibility,

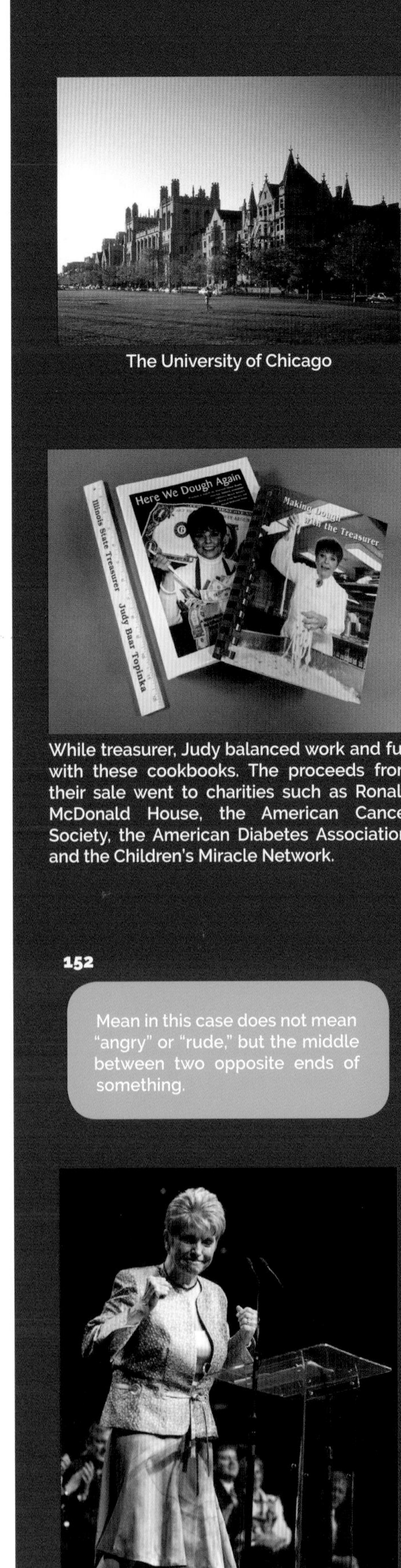

The University of Chicago

While treasurer, Judy balanced work and fun with these cookbooks. The proceeds from their sale went to charities such as Ronald McDonald House, the American Cancer Society, the American Diabetes Association, and the Children's Miracle Network.

152 Mean in this case does not mean "angry" or "rude," but the middle between two opposite ends of something.

Judy at her final inauguration

and you have to be very, very careful about not "overdrawing." Taking money out of a bank account and spending it is very easy compared to earning the money and putting it into a bank account. This is true with integrity. It is easy to take trust out and lose it with others, but it is very hard to replace it.

Judy earned a lot of trust from the citizens of Illinois, including those within both the Republican and Democratic parties. People could count on her word being her bond and, if she could not keep a promise, she would tell you up front that she could not make the promise. During phone calls with her son while she was running for governor, Judy used to tell Joe how people offered her campaign donations in exchange for a promise for something in return if she won the election. She would not make those promises and found herself with fewer donations because of that integrity. She told Joe she was not going to encourage the "pay to play" mentality. If people wanted a leader who cared and would try her best, they should donate. If not, then she would lose the election but lose on her own terms.

What are your most important values and moral principles? What are some ways that you make sure your behavior matches these beliefs? What do you do in situations where it is hard to maintain your integrity—to be honest and trustworthy? Think about a time you made a bad choice in this area; how did you go about fixing it? Ask your friends, family members, and other adults you know about what integrity and honesty mean to them. How do their responses compare to what you expected to hear? Do their responses give you new ideas about practicing integrity?

People face situations every day that can test their trustworthiness, and the consequences of a poor decision can affect a person for the rest of his or her life. Judy was known to repeat quotations and old sayings while Joe was growing up. One of her favorites was often used by Benjamin Franklin: "Honesty is the best policy."[153] That pretty much summed up Judy's approach to living and it's a good one for all of us. Keep it in mind as you grow up and decide how you wish to live your life.

153

While this quote is in Franklin's book *Poor Richard's Almanack*, there is debate about its origins previous to Franklin's publication.

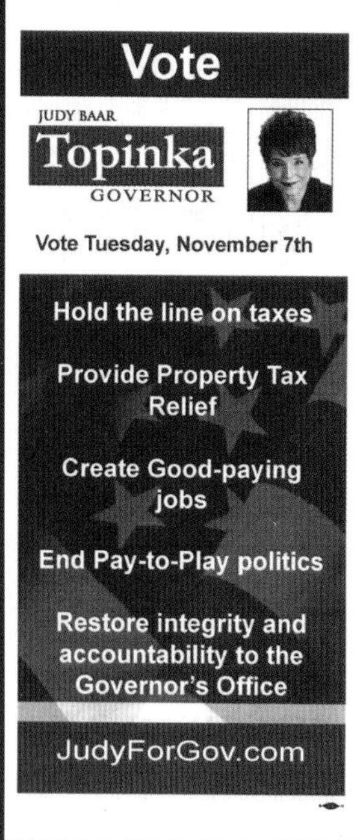

Vote
JUDY BAAR
Topinka
GOVERNOR
Vote Tuesday, November 7th
Hold the line on taxes
Provide Property Tax Relief
Create Good-paying jobs
End Pay-to-Play politics
Restore integrity and accountability to the Governor's Office
JudyForGov.com

Judy mentioned integrity in one of her campaign brochures.

Heritage

Heritage refers to the traditions, culture, practices, and beliefs that we get from our relatives, friends, and communities. Sometimes it is tied to our ethnic backgrounds. Other times, it comes from our religious beliefs. Czech, Slovak, Mexican, African-American, Korean, Catholic, Jewish, Muslim...we are all in this together. We all have diverse backgrounds because we live in a country that is made up primarily of immigrants. Where we and our families come from, and the ways that we live and what we believe that are different from others, are part of our heritage, but so are the things we have in common as Americans.

Judy understood this importance of heritage—and unity in diversity—her whole life. It started when she was a child learning her family's roots and how it made her different. She had great pride in her Czech and Slovak background, and she occasionally took a ribbing for it, as when she played the accordion or spoke in a strange language. But, because Judy appreciated her own heritage, she could also appreciate the ethnic backgrounds of others and the strong sense of pride that often accompany them. She would dress in her Czech kroj (sounds like kroy)[154] at Czech functions, but she would wear a sari (sounds like sorry) at Indian events, a dirndl (sounds like durn-dl) at German events, or an áo dài (sounds like ow-dye) dress at Vietnamese events. And, like all Chicago politicians, she was known to wear a lot of green at Irish celebrations—especially at the St. Patrick's Day parade in Chicago. She spoke Czech as her first language and English as her second language, but she could also get by with French, Spanish, Polish, and a little German. If she couldn't speak a group's language, she tried her best to learn some special words and use them within public settings to become closer to people and their cultures.

For Judy, everyone was in this world together no matter their religion, ethnic background, age, gender, sexual preference, or sexual identity. Togetherness was her watchword. We could have pride in each other's differences, and we could have

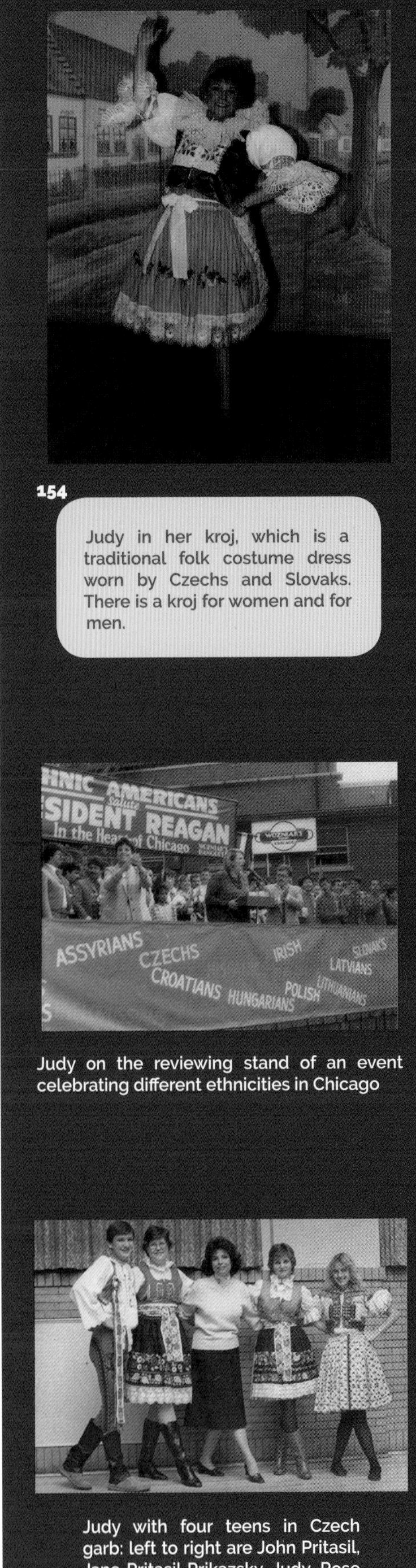

154

Judy in her kroj, which is a traditional folk costume dress worn by Czechs and Slovaks. There is a kroj for women and for men.

Judy on the reviewing stand of an event celebrating different ethnicities in Chicago

Judy with four teens in Czech garb: left to right are John Pritasil, Jane Pritasil Prikazsky, Judy, Rose Pritasil, and Irene Balas

Judy in her kroj during the annual Houby parade on Cermak Road. The parade is still held yearly in Cicero and Berwyn.

Judy almost never missed a Fourth of July parade. She rode this elephant float in 1982.

pride in being citizens of a great state and a great country. Our differences made us stronger and made Illinois and the United States the best places in the world to live. Judy was proud of being a citizen of the United States, and being an American was her favorite part of her unique heritage.

What is your heritage, and why is it important to you? Is it any more or less important than someone else's background? Ask your friends about their family's roots and tell them about yours. If you'd like to know more about your family's background, there are lots of resources online and at the library to help.

What does your American heritage mean to you? In a world that is so connected today, is there a collective, global heritage? Never be ashamed of who you are, and applaud other's pride in who they are. Being united, even with our differences, is part of our culture as citizens of the greatest "melting pot"[155] in history, the United States of America.

155 "Melting pot" is a concept where people from different cultures come together to form one group. It is often used to describe how immigrants with different backgrounds come to the United States and become part of the United States as citizens.

Advocacy

Advocacy means supporting a cause or proposal. It also refers to speaking up or out about something you like or do not like because you believe it is right or wrong. Judy loved being a citizen of the United States because the country gave her the right to speak up, and it gave her the opportunity to run and win elected office, where her voice was that much louder, representing many more people than just herself. Judy spoke up for those she represented as well as for those things that particularly mattered to her, like the rights of veterans, especially those with disabilities; the rights of reservist and National Guard personnel when they were deployed; the rights of orphans seeking families that were not necessarily traditional families but were loving all the same; and the rights of social organizations just trying to pay their bills so they could survive and support others throughout Illinois.

Sometimes Judy could be blunt and cause others great discomfort in her candor, but normally it was because she was right and they were wrong. In a world where people do not

State Rep Judy in a committee hearing

answer questions or provide disclosure, Judy would "tell it as it is" and people came to expect nothing less from her.

What are issues and beliefs that you are passionate about and that you think are important for your community, state, and country today and in the future? How can you advocate for those things now? How might you pursue these issues and beliefs as you grow older? Judy never lost her sense of herself and always had the courage to speak up for the things that mattered to her and to others. Judy expected others to tell it as it is and fight for what they believed. Will you advocate for the things that matter to you? You can always come back to Judy's life and story for inspiration.

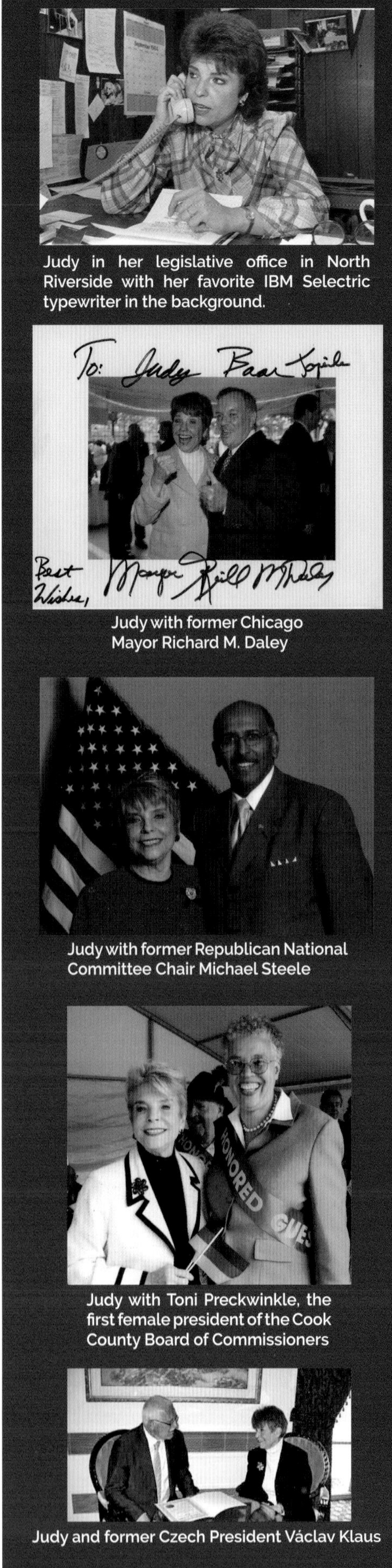

Judy in her legislative office in North Riverside with her favorite IBM Selectric typewriter in the background.

Judy with former Chicago Mayor Richard M. Daley

Judy with former Republican National Committee Chair Michael Steele

Judy with Toni Preckwinkle, the first female president of the Cook County Board of Commissioners

Judy and former Czech President Václav Klaus

Anton Cermak Kerner
Chicago, Illinois

October 21, 2017

Dear Reader:

My grandfather, Anton Cermak (1873-1933), was perhaps the most famous Czech-American politician to precede my grandfather, Illinois Attorney General Otto Kerner Sr. (1884-1952), my father, Illinois Governor Otto Kerner Jr. (1908-1976), and my friend, Illinois Comptroller Judy Baar Topinka (1944-2014). Like Judy's grandparents, Cermak pursued the American dream when he immigrated to the United States. Cermak worked in the coal mines of Illinois alongside his father. Cermak was elected mayor of Chicago in 1931 and, like Judy, he began his public service in Illinois state government.

As a politician, Cermak helped to create the pan-ethnic, labor-based, Cook County Democratic Party which helped to elect Franklin Roosevelt President of the United States in 1932. Like Judy, who worked for President Ronald Reagan's Ethnics for Reagan campaign, Cermak and the Kerners all understood that we each - whether Czech, Polish, German, African-American, Latin-American, Catholic, Jew, Muslim, etc. - are stronger when our neighborhoods, our cities, our counties, and our states stand together. Anton Cermak brought people together, and he inspired people like the Otto Kerners and Judy Baar Topinkas to do the same. More information about Cermak and Otto Kerner Sr. can be found at http://www.friendsofbnc.org/. Both are interred at Bohemian National Cemetery in Chicago.

I hope you have enjoyed reading this book about Judy Baar Topinka. She was an incredible woman who represented her Czech heritage always with pride and loved her village, township, county, legislative and senate districts, state, and country to the end. She looked up to my father and my grandfathers as role models and lived like they did, facing the successes, obstacles, and tragedies of political life, never giving up on her constituents despite whatever she faced. She is a role model for us all.

Sbohem Judy. Až se znovu setkáme.

Sincerely,

Anton Cermak Kerner

Anton Cermak Kerner

Goodbye Judy. Until we meet again.

CERMAK

Former Czech Minister of Foreign Affairs Lubomír Zaorálek laying flowers at the Cermak family mausoleum at Bohemian National Cemetery in Chicago

Resources for Further Research

Judy's family has set up The Judy Baar Topinka Charitable Foundation. Its website is at http://www.judybaartopinka.org/. The family is constantly adding news things to the site, including photographs and streaming videos of Judy.

Judy loved quotes from Benjamin Franklin. Proverbs and aphorisms from Benjamin Franklin's Poor Richard's Almanack can be found at https://www.poorrichards.net.

Information about the Lyric Opera of Chicago is located at https://www.lyricopera.org.

Information about the Chicago Symphony Orchestra is located at http://cso.org.

Explore culture in Illinois further at http://www.enjoyillinois.com.

The University of Chicago's Slavic/Eastern Europe/Eurasia Studies collections can be found at http://guides.lib.uchicago.edu/slavic.

The Pritzker Military Museum and Library is a wonderful place to visit. Information is located at http://www.pritzkermilitary.org. Judy donated so many military treasures from her estate sales to this museum.

Judy visited the United Nations once as a child in the 1950s and then as an adult with her son in the early part of this century. She never lost her faith in a global community, and she never lost her faith in the United Nations. Read about the United Nations at http://www.un.org/en/index.html but, more importantly, explore its member states at http://www.un.org/en/member-states/index.html. The world is so big. Take the time to learn what you can about its cultures and peoples!

Civics Project Ideas and Classroom Learning Activities

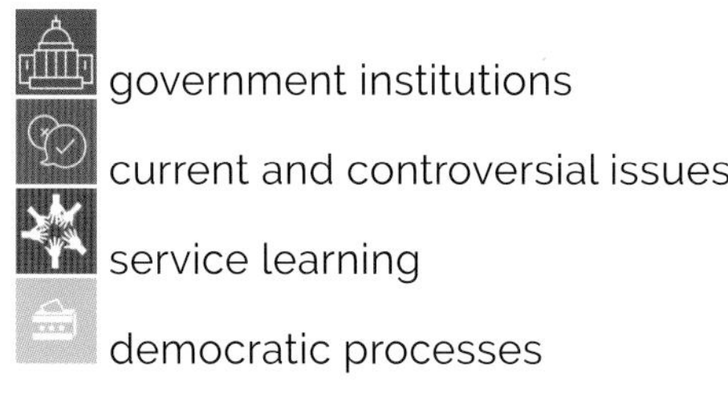

Chapter 10 Key Concepts:

- Management and Leadership
- Civility, Protocol, and Compromise
- Perseverance
- Balance
- Integrity
- Heritage
- Advocacy

Chapter 10 Classroom Activities (Teacher):

- Reflect on the life, characteristics, and values of Judy Baar Topinka with your students. What stands out most for them? Ask students to pick one of her characteristics that resonates most for them. Why does it matter to them? How does that characteristic or value relate to each of their own lives?
- Explore with students what it means to be a public servant. Is it important to help others by being in government? Do they ever think about running for office someday? Which one? Why or why not?

Chapter 10 Essay Topics (Student):

- What did you like about Judy Baar Topinka? What did you not like about her? What can you learn from her life and apply to your life?
- If Judy Baar Topinka were alive today, what would you say to her? What do you think she may say to you?
- Pick one of the key concepts from this chapter and write about why you think that concept was important for Judy Baar Topinka and how it could be important for you as you grow older.

Acknowledgments

My hope is that when you read about Judy Baar Topinka, you will see many qualities of her character and examples from her life that you can adopt in your own life. I am not alone in this wish, and I want to thank those who have shared in this vision and helped in their own way to make this book a reality. One such person is Colonel Jennifer Pritzker, who thought the world of Judy—and Judy thought the world of her. Another is Hilton Hudson, the president of Hilton Publishing. He reminds me so much of my mother. Still another is my writing coach, Sharon Woodhouse, who is an incredible editor and such a wonderful supporter. Four others are Jim Nosek, James Connally, Mike Maciejewski, and Anton Kerner, who always listened to me and were there to help me bring together so many stories and materials. I also need to thank my best friends from high school and college, Vicki Dvorak Isely and Krista Walsh Matlock, who never left my side for decades despite the craziness of my mother's political life and my military life. And finally, there is my wife, Christina, who personally hopes that Judy's story will inspire so many young people, including our daughter, Alexandra Faith Baar Topinka. Alexandra talks about Judy, whom she knew as Babi. She will always miss Judy, but she will always have her grandmother's story as a role model.

About the Author

Joseph Baar Topinka is the only son of Judy Baar Topinka. He was born in Berwyn, Illinois, and grew up in neighboring Riverside, where he attended the same junior high school as his mother. He learned about government and Illinois politics firsthand while his mother learned about them as a state legislator in the 1980s and 1990s. Her desire to be a public servant inspired him to also pursue a career in public service. He joined the Reserve Officer Training Corps in college and then was commissioned as an officer in the Illinois Army National Guard at the University of Illinois at Champaign-Urbana in 1990. After graduating from the College of Law at Northern Illinois University in 1993, he entered active duty as an attorney in the U.S. Army's Judge Advocate General's Corps.

Joe may have been stationed hundreds or thousands of miles away, but he was always close to his mother when needed, and he always stayed up to date about what was going on back home. Like his mother, he was always proud of his home state of Illinois, even during some rocky times in its political history. Joe retired from the U.S. Army in 2014 after acquiring four more degrees. Like his mom, he never stopped learning and growing. He had hoped that after leaving the U.S. Army, his daughter, Alexandra, his wife, Christina, and he would have more time with Judy. Unfortunately, she passed away a few months after his retirement. In order to honor Judy's legacy, Joe and Christina founded *The Judy Baar Topinka Charitable Foundation*, whose purpose is to support leadership, education, and training for young men and women with demonstrated involvement in public affairs.

Image Credits

1. "First Iwo Jima Flag Raising" by SSgt Louis R. Lowery, USMC. As a work of the U.S. federal government, this image is in the public domain.
3. "Flag of Cook County" by Daniel X. O'Neil is licensed under CC BY 2.0 / Cropped from original
4. "Imperial Coat of Arms of the Empire of Austria" by Sodacan is licensed under CC BY-SA 3.0
13. "Portrait of Frederick Law Olmstead" by James Notman. As its first publication occurred prior to January 1, 1923, this image is in the public domain.
29. "Alois Jirásek" by Jan Vilímek. As the author died more than 70 years ago, this image is in the public domain. Cropped from original.
33. Sokol logo used with permission of American Sokol.
34. "Joseph Medill" by unknown author. As the author died more than 70 years ago, this image is in the public domain.
36. "Image 6727 Riverside" by Boscophotos is licensed under CC BY-SA 3.0
41. "American Medical Association HQ" by Pinotgris is licensed under CC BY-SA 3.0
42. "Chicago Elevated Train" by Marcel"lazytom"Marchon is licensed under CC BY-SA 2.0
43. "Metra City of Woodstock in Deerfield" by keelysam is licensed under CC BY-SA 2.5
44. "Topinky" by Geolina163 is licensed under CC BY-SA 3.0
45. "Night view of the Castle and Charles Bridge, Prague, Czech Republic," © Jorge Royan / http://www.royan.com.ar / CC BY-SA 3.0
48. "Seal of the United States Navy," "Seal of the United States Marine Corps," "Seal of the United States Army," and "Seal of the United States Air Force" are works of the U.S. federal government and are in the public domain.
50. "Moravia" illustrated by Lukáš Mižoch. According to the Czech Copyright Act, this work is in the public domain.

p. 33 "Illinois House of Representatives" by Daniel Schwen is licensed under CC BY-SA 4.0

52. "Emblem of the Papacy" by Cronholm144, derived from a work by Hautala, who created the work from Open Clip Art Library. The author has released this work into the public domain.
53. "Ihs-logo" by unknown author; illustrated by Moranski. As the author died more than 70 years ago, this image is in the public domain.

54. “Parliament at Sunset” by Mike Gimelfarb. The author has released this work into the public domain.

56. “Coat of arms of Czechoslovakia (1961-1989)” by PavelD is licensed under CC BY-SA 3.0

63. “elephant-964294” by InspiredImages is licensed under CC0; “america-2025465” by OpenClipart-Vectors is licensed under CC0

69. “Illinois State Capitol” by Teemu008 is licensed under CC BY-SA 2.0

93. “Lyndon LaRouche” by Museras is licensed under CC BY-SA 3.0

p. 53 “JimEdgar2013” by W. Wadas/Éovart Caçeir is licensed under CC BY-SA 3.0 / Cropped from original

94. “William B. Ogden” by George Peter Alexander Healy. As the copyright term is the author's life plus 100 years or less, this image is in the public domain.

107. “2003 IL Proof” is a work of the U.S. federal government, is ineligible for U.S. copyright, and is therefore in the public domain in the United States.

108. “USA grants tomb” by Daniel Schwen is licensed under CC BY-SA 3.0

109. “Central Illinois Prairie” by Ron Frazier is licensed under CC BY 2.0 / Cropped from original

p. 60 “Blagojevichmayor” by SSgt Michelle Ingram, USAF. Cropped from original. As a work of the U.S. federal government, this image is in the public domain.

p. 60 “Dirksen United States Courthouse, Chicago Loop, Chicago, Illinois” by Ken Lund is licensed under CC BY-SA 2.0

p. 60 “FCIEnglewoodLarge” is a work prepared by an officer or employee of the United States government as part of that person's official duties and is therefore in the public domain.

112. “Alan Keyes” by Rich Girard is licensed under CC BY-SA 2.0

113. “Official Senate Portrait of Barack Obama (D-IL)” is a work of the U.S. federal government and is in the public domain.

115. “Klas Restaurant” by charlie vinz is licensed under CC BY-SA 2.0 / Cropped from original

p. 67 Photo of Blythe Park School used with permission of Riverside School District 96.

130. Clapperboard by OpenClipart-Vectors is licensed under CC0

131. “Loyola University Chicago sign on Sheridan Ave” by Amerique is licensed under CC BY 3.0

143. Courtroom photo by Pixabay user 12019 is licensed under CC0

p. 80 “Tootsie-Roll-WU” by Evan-Amos is licensed under CC BY-SA 3.0 / Background made transparent and candies moved closer together

p. 80 “Vienna Beef Hot Dogs Sign at the Chicago River on Wacker” by Daniel X. O'Neil is licensed under CC BY 2.0 / Cropped from original

p. 80 Eli's Cheesecake logo used with permission of Marc Schulman.

147. “Margaret Brown, 3qtr view, with chair” by Bain News Service. Available from the George Grantham Bain collection at the United States Library of Congress's Prints and Photographs division. There are

no known copyright restrictions on the photographs in the George Grantham Bain collection.

147. "RMS Titanic 3" is in the public domain in the United States because it was published (or registered with the U.S. Copyright Office) before January 1, 1923.

151. "Greetings from Peoria, Ill." by Tichnor Brothers. This work is in the public domain in the United States because it was published in the United States between 1923 and 1977 without a copyright notice.

153. "Portrait of Benjamin Franklin" by Henry Bryan Hall (engraving of original painting by Joseph Duplessis). This is a faithful photographic reproduction of a two-dimensional, public domain work of art. The work of art itself is in the public domain in its country of origin and other countries and areas where the copyright term is the author's life plus 100 years or less.